IMAGES
of America

ATLANTIC CITY
REVISITED

The Absecon Lighthouse consisted of 228 steps up a spiral stairway to the lookout platform and another 12 steps to the light room. Electricity was used in the lighthouse for the first time in 1925. The lighthouse was originally built on the high dune line, but erosion threatened the structure. Jetties were built to shore it up, and eventually, accretion created enough land for streets and houses between the lighthouse and the coast. As Atlantic City grew in popularity, the lighthouse had plenty of neighbors growing up around it, threatening its effectiveness. High-rise hotels along the boardwalk also made it difficult for ship captains to see the beam. As a result, it lost its usefulness. A steel tower built at New Hampshire Avenue and the boardwalk in 1933 served as a replacement for the lighthouse. Shortly afterward, the federal government decommissioned the lighthouse and extinguished its lamp. It remains the tallest urban lighthouse in the country.

On the cover: Crowds gather on the beach and boardwalk for the Traymore Hotel's Mark Twain Memorial Huckleberry Finn Contest, in which hundreds of boys donned hats and poles and competed, sans shoes, in a look-alike contest in the 1930s. (Courtesy of Robert E. Ruffolo Jr.)

IMAGES
of America

ATLANTIC CITY
REVISITED

William H. Sokolic
and Robert E. Ruffolo Jr.

ARCADIA
PUBLISHING

Published by Arcadia Publishing
Charleston, South Carolina

Library of Congress Catalog Card Number: 2006931757

For all general information contact Arcadia Publishing at:
Telephone 843-853-2070
Fax 843-853-0044
E-mail sales@arcadiapublishing.com
For customer service and orders:
Toll-Free 1-888-313-2665

Visit us on the Internet at www.arcadiapublishing.com

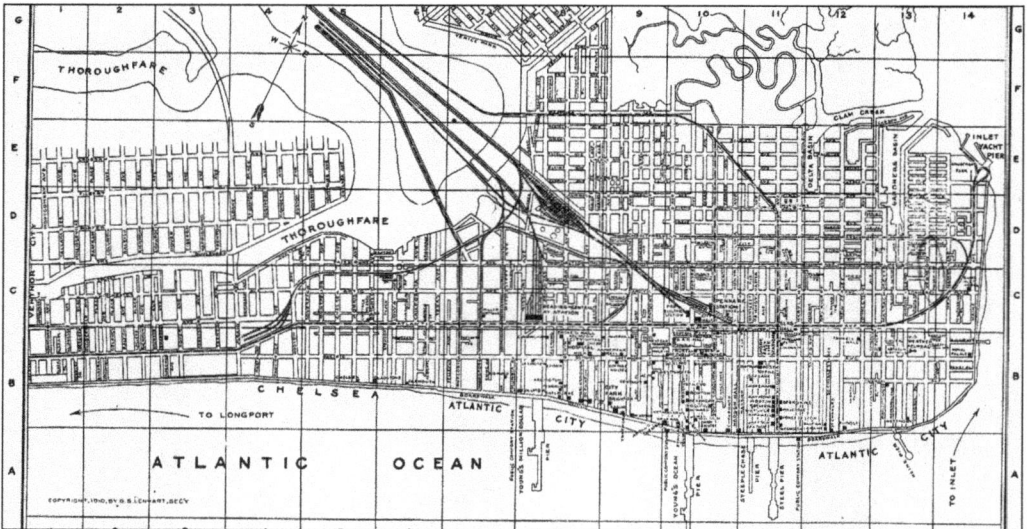

This 1910 map shows a thriving resort, with an extensive transportation system. The city was fed by two railroads, the Reading-Central and the Pennsylvania. Trolley service brought visitors throughout the city, as did sedans, the precursor to jitneys. More than 10,000 hotel rooms (not including the rooming houses and guesthouses) served the populace who arrived by train. This map lists the rail and trolley lines, the Reading Central terminal at Arkansas Avenue, and the Pennsylvania terminal at South Carolina Avenue. Also shown are the piers and hotels.

CONTENTS

ACKNOWLEDGMENTS

For their contributions and insight, we would like to thank Boo Pergament, Tom Hulme, Henry White, Anthony Kutschera, Redenia Gilliam-Mosee, Mike Cohen, Tom Allen, Howard Kyle, Joe Genova, Ann Bunting, Tony Scola, Bill Burch, Ed Oldfield, William Conover, Herb and Faith Stern, Lillian Levy, Vicki Gold Levi, George and Mary Kirlin, Donna Connor, Stephen Piccolo, Hoag Levins, David G. Schwartz, Murray Raphel, and Rod Aluise.

We are also indebted to Paul Siemiemkowicz for his assistance in scanning the images, and to everyone at Princeton Antiques Bookshop who also worked on this project: Joyce, Robert Anthony, Jake, Daniel and Antonio Ruffolo, Terry Dayton, Susan Comis, Micah Kurtz, and Christine Albertson.

The following organizations were invaluable: Atlantic City Historical Museum; Atlantic City Free Public Library; African American Heritage Museum of Southern New Jersey; Noyes Museum; Committee to Restore Pop Lloyd Field; the Miss America Organization; National Register of Historic Places; the National Park Service; Wikipedia; Chicken Bone Beach Historical Foundation; the New Jersey Casino Control Commission; Atlantic City Convention Hall Organ Society; Inlet Public/Private Association; the National Trust; the Baseball Hall of Fame; and Atlantic City casinos.

We are indebted to the following books: *We Had A Shore Fast Line*, by Mervin Borgnis; *The Book Of The Boardwalk*, by Frank Butler; *Rum Row*, by Robert Carse; *Atlantic City Diary*, by Ed Davis; *By The Beautiful Sea*, by Charles Funnell; *The Sea Bright Skiff and Other Shore Boats*, by Peter Guthorn; *Absegami Annals of Eyren Haven and Atlantic City*, by Alfred Heston; *Atlantic City, America's Playground*, by Bill Kent, Lauralee Dobbins, and Robert E. Ruffolo; *The Boardwalk*, by Robert Kotlowitz; *Atlantic City: 125 Years of Ocean Madness*, by Vicky Gold Levi and Lee Eisenberg; *The Company That Bought the Boardwalk: About How Resorts International Came To Atlantic City*, by Gigi Mahon; *So Young, So Gay! Story of the Boardwalk*, by William McMahon; *Boardwalk Memories*, by Emil R. Salvini; *Arts & Crafts to Modern Design: William L. Price*, by George E. Thomas; and *Boardwalk of Dreams: Atlantic City and the Fate of Urban America*, by Bryant Simon

A nod to these Web sites for their help: www.deanmartinfancenter.com; www.jerrylewiscomedy. com; www.squashtalk.com; and www.rarebeatles.com.

We would also like to thank in memoriam those who have educated us on Atlantic City history: Sid Schrier, Jack Bradley, Sonora Carver, Arnette and Jake French, Sid Trusty, Willie D'Amato, Fred and Betty Earhart, Florence and George Miller, and Adrian and Don Phillips.

INTRODUCTION

Before Atlantic City was Atlantic City, and before its streets became fodder for Monopoly, it was known as Absegami, or Absecon Island, to the Native Americans. It was not the hospitable place it is today, or even a 100 years ago; high natural dunes, dense vegetation, black snakes, and mosquitoes ruled the area. Still, Jeremiah Leeds did not find it a turnoff when he became the first settler in 1838, building a cabin in what later became Baltic Avenue.

By 1850, a handful of folks joined Leeds on the island. But it was mainland resident Dr. Jonathan Pitney and Philadelphia civil engineer Richard Osborne who saw the future. Pitney and Osborne teamed up to convince investors to buy shares in the Camden and Atlantic Railroad, which would carry Philadelphians to the New Jersey coast. Osborne drew a straight line from Camden to the shore, and after discussing a number of names for this newly minted paradise, he settled on Atlantic City.

For a small community, Atlantic City has had a major impact on the American cultural landscape since its inception. This book will focus on that impact by picturing the chronological evolution of the resort, from its fabrication by railroad people bent on bringing the masses from Philadelphia to the sea, to its rise as the gaming capital of the East Coast.

In July 1854, with the rail line ready and a city charter approved by the governor of New Jersey, the first train pulled out of Camden bound for Atlantic City. The train made it as far as the tip of the bay, where passengers hopped a boat to the island. A few months later, the bridge over the bay opened and the rail line was complete.

Hotels and rooming houses followed the coming of the railroad, the most notable of which was the massive 600-room United States Hotel. By 1860, 4,000 tourists visited Atlantic City in the summer, attracted by the promise of a cure for all manner of ailments. The city thrived. In 1870, the first boardwalk made its appearance. The final version—the one in place today—was built before the end of the 19th century.

As the 20th century began, Atlantic City became America's premiere resort, but one where working-class Philadelphians and the crème of main line society coexisted in a de facto, symbiotic relationship. The resort grew up mostly between the two world wars. The Miss America Pageant debuted in 1921 as a publicity stunt to expand the tourist season. Convention hall opened as an architectural marvel. Monopoly first appeared in the 1930s, the product of an out-of-work Philadelphian, named Charles Darrow, who used Atlantic City's streets as the backdrop of the popular game. The city also played a key role during World War II when the armed services all but commandeered it.

The growing popularity of air travel in the 1950s and 1960s and the aging of its grand hotels brought Atlantic City to a gradual decline. The final death knell, however, was sounded during the Democratic National Convention in 1964; with the nomination of Lyndon B. Johnson a lock, the national media turned its attention to the city itself, and the reports were not pretty. This picture served as the face of Atlantic City until legalized gambling arrived in 1978 with the opening of the Resorts International Casino Hotel.

A succession of political bosses ran the resort until the early 1970s. During Prohibition, these bosses insured that the booze flowed freely and openly, while other cities were forced to hide their liquor behind speakeasy doors. The black population, mostly living north of Atlantic Avenue, provided a constant source of employment for hotels with grand names such as Chalfonte-Haddon Hall, Marlborough-Blenheim, Traymore, and Shelburne. While tourism and gaming have marked Atlantic City's reason for being through much of its existence, the city also evolved into the surf clam capital of the United States. Its fleet of boats rakes in the majority of clams used in sauces and soups, and more than two-thirds of the clams consumed in the world come through New Jersey ports.

Atlantic City must also be credited for a number of firsts. In addition to Miss America and Monopoly, the city gave birth to the rolling chair, saltwater taffy, the jitney, and even the picture postcard. The resort made the amusement pier famous with Garden Pier, Steel Pier, and Million Dollar Pier, among others. The term airport was coined at the city's Bader Field.

With its huge vacationing visitors base, Broadway tapped Atlantic City as the most important tryout locale due to its many theaters. Dean Martin and Jerry Lewis paired up for the first time at the famed 500 Club. Almost every major musical and comic act played Steel Pier and the variety of nightclubs throughout the city. The convention hall hosted indoor football long before domed stadiums, the Beatles, the Rolling Stones, the Democrats, and, until 2006, the Miss America Pageant.

And of course, there is the boardwalk itself, a street like no other in the world and one the gaming industry had belatedly come to recognize as a resource to be used, along with the beach. The four-mile long boardwalk stretches from the inlet to the Ventnor border and is chock full of the glitzy and the schmaltzy. In its 100-plus years of service, it has been home to fast-food joints and classy restaurants, fortune-tellers and expensive jewelry stores, hucksters and hipsters. T-shirt emporiums and junky souvenir shops, pizza parlors and fudge and taffy shops, and arcades and amusement rides, which stand side by side with the elegance of the casinos.

With gaming, the city rose from its own ashes as the first place outside Nevada to offer legal gambling in the United States. Gaming succeeded beyond even the most optimistic projections of its supporters. By 1990, a dozen casinos operated in Atlantic City. They created a 24/7 year-round industry, not one bound by just the 10 weeks between Memorial Day and Labor Day. Garish and opulent casino hotels replaced many of the boardwalk dowagers, and new palaces opened in the once-desolate marina section of town.

By 1990, when the Taj Mahal opened as the tallest building in New Jersey, many of the casinos adapted the same faded look as their pre-gaming predecessors. The old look still attracted visitors the city and the casinos still raked in more money every year. But less than five years later, the threat of gambling in neighboring states brought in Las Vegas casino operators seeking to raise the bar beyond the bus-and-buffet crowd. Borgata Hotel Casino and Spa opened in 2003 and triggered a renaissance, the Tropicana launched the Quarter, Caesar's added the Pier at Caesar's, and Showboat partnered with the House of Blues.

And the future is limitless.

One

Rising to
the Occasion
1854–1920

"Build it and they will come." Indeed they did. After the launch of the Camden and Atlantic Railroad, a direct link from Camden to the coast, the newly named Atlantic City took off as a popular resort for those from the Philadelphia area. Although the locale originally consisted of dunes, mosquitoes, snakes, and a handful of settlers, the city eventually grew to attract everyone from presidents to janitors. Hotels joined boardinghouses to accommodate the throng of visitors. The United States Hotel was the largest of its kind when it opened soon after the introduction of rail service. The Absecon Lighthouse opened just three years later, designed to warn ships of the treacherous inlets. The boardwalk evolved from a wooden doormat to keep sand out of hotel lobbies and train cars to a merchant thoroughfare as shops, restaurants, and businesses rose along its wooden way. Hotels like the Traymore and Marlborough-Blenheim rose from modest beginnings as rooming houses into architectural marvels. Piers grew up and down Atlantic City like fingers on a hand. Young's, Steeplechase, and Steel Piers all arrived before the 20th century. The nation's first paid lifeguard even debuted in Atlantic City. Rolling chairs and saltwater taffy were two other local innovations, along with a unique form of transport known as jitneys.

The idea was simple enough: draw a straight line from Camden to the coast, lay track, and bring the masses from Philadelphia and South Jersey to the shore for respite on what the Native Americans called Absegami, or Absecon Island. Dr. Jonathan Pitney, a physician living near the coast, pitched this idea to engineer Richard Osborne. In turn, Osborne pitched it to investors, and the result was the Camden and Atlantic Railroad. The company received its charter in 1852. The train made its inaugural run on July 1, 1854, carrying officials, newspaper people, and invited guests over the Delaware River by ferry, and through the rural midsection of South Jersey. It ended its journey on the mainland, across the bay from what the railroaders named Atlantic City. From there, a ferry carted the visitors to the island where another train would take them up Atlantic Avenue to the United States Hotel. The entire trip took two and a half hours. With the subsequent completion of the bridge over the beach thoroughfare, trains rode directly into the city.

P. R. R. Station, Atlantic City, N. J.

Regularly scheduled train service began on July 4, 1854. The first rail station was built at North Carolina and Atlantic Avenues. The station was moved to New Hampshire Avenue in 1876. The Camden and Atlantic Railroad eventually became the Pennsylvania Railroad, as the city grew from its initial collection of occasional boardinghouses and scattered shacks amid sand dunes, snakes, and mosquitoes. Atlantic City attracted a mixed demographic to its door; ladies in their finest gowns and men in their suits mingled with the lower working classes at this railroad terminal. All were attracted to what Richard Osborne called Philadelphia's lungs.

11

UNITED STATES HOTEL, ATLANTIC CITY; BROWN & WOELPPER, OWNERS AND PROPRIETORS.

Richard Osborne is credited with laying out the streets. Cross streets were named after states and the others after the oceans of the world. At Atlantic, Pacific, Delaware, and Maryland Avenues stood what was one of the largest hotels in the country. The United State Hotel, built by the Camden and Atlantic Railroad, rose four stories and featured, gardens, sunporches, and 600 guest rooms. Train tracks ran in front of the hotel to bring guests to and from the rail terminal. Mule trains took people to the beach, which was almost a block away. The hotel brought in its share of dignitaries from the outset when Ulysses S. Grant stayed at the United States. It was not the only hotel in Atlantic City during the early years, however. The Mansion House, Congress Hall, and the Surf House also provided lodging for visitors. Eventually, the hotels were demolished, but their past is reflected in States Avenue, which cut through the United States Hotel site and Congress Avenue, where Congress Hall lay.

No sooner had the railroad established Atlantic City then efforts were under way to convince the federal government of the need for a lighthouse on the northern end of the island, to warn ships of the treacherous waters and shoals of Absecon Inlet. With approvals in hand, civil engineer George G. Meade designed and built the Absecon Lighthouse in 1856 at Rhode Island and Pacific Avenues. A year later, the light atop the 167-foot structure turned on, casting a beam 20 miles out to sea. Several years later, Meade went on to fame in another arena: as commander of the victorious Union Army at the battle of Gettysburg in 1863.

The initial reason for Atlantic City's founding lay in the salt waters of the Atlantic and the wide beaches that fronted the ocean. Dr. Jonathan Pitney and others touted the curative powers of the briny Atlantic. Crowds sunbathed on the sand in attire deemed appropriate by authorities. Men and women were required to cover all parts of the body except face and hands; men had to wear shirts until 1940. At one point, the city employed beach censors to ensure that excessive skin was not exposed. Early bathers wore bathing dresses of wool flannel with stockings, canvas shoes, and large straw hats. The more-daring bloomer suits and stockings worn by the bathing beauties on the left were not introduced until 1907.

Atlantic City organized the first paid beach patrol in the nation in 1892. Prior to that, volunteers patrolled the beach, or hotels hired their own. The outfits seen in the postcard changed little over the early years. The badge on the tank-top jersey spoke of the police powers granted to lifeguards in those days to monitor behavior problems and improper dress and conduct.

A LIFE GUARD   ATLANTIC CITY, N.J.

The lifeguards in this image pose adjacent to their lifeboats in the early years of the 20th century. During these years, there were no stations on the beach. Lifeguards rowed boats or walked up and down the beach, on patrol. Harry and Stanley Van Sant made lifeboats before 1900. Later the Van Duyne brothers used the same style in fiberglass.

15

Atlantic City established a relationship with nascent aviation. In 1910, the Atlantic City Air Carnival began a 10-day run. Glenn H. Curtiss, whose biplane is pictured here on the beach, set a world's record for time by flying 50 miles back and forth for an hour and 14 minutes. Curtiss also performed the first bombing demonstration from an airplane during the carnival, dropping oranges and other fruit on the beach.

In 1910, polar explorer Walter Wellman left Atlantic City in the dirigible *America* hoping to fly across the Atlantic. But 1,000 miles out to sea, storms forced the crew to abandon ship. Two years later, Wellman's mechanic, Melvin Vaniman, readied the dirigible *Akron*, for another attempt. The ship rose over the inlet before an explosion dropped the airship and its crew into the sea, killing all (including Vaniman).

16

The beginning of the 20th century brought high-rise hotels, which became the foundations for the grand dames of Atlantic City in its initial heyday during the first half of the 20th century. The city developed a skyline. The photograph above, from 1916, features the Royal Palace Hotel in the inlet at Pacific Avenue and the ocean. The bottom image shows the Dunlop Hotel on Ocean Avenue toward the left. Just to the right of the center is the Chalfonte Hotel, which evolved from an 1868 boardinghouse to the first fireproof and iron-framed hotel in the city when it opened in 1904.

HOTEL TRAYMORE
Atlantic City

DINNER DE LUXE

$2.50 INCLUSIVE OF A COCKTAIL AND WINE

FEBRUARY 22, 1917

STERLING POINT OYSTER COCKTAIL

STSCHI A LA LIVONIENNE
OU
POTAGE FLORENTINE

SUPREME DE SOLE DUGUESCLIN

POITRINE DE VOLAILLE POMPADOUR
SALADE TRAYMORE

COUPE DE CERISES BLANCHES WASHINGTON
DESIRS DE DAMES

DEMI TASSE

The hotels in Atlantic City prided themselves on their culinary expertise. The image to the left shows the Traymore menu from the winter of 1917. The courses, written mostly in French, ranged from appetizer to dessert for $2.50 a person, including wine and a cocktail. The bottom image depicts the Brighton Hotel, famous for its popular Brighton Punch. A closely guarded recipe, the drink was said to pack such a wallop that women were allowed only two glasses a day. The photograph of the Brighton Hotel, just off the boardwalk, includes the aptly named Brighton Park, a garden owned by Brighton owner George F. Lee and Hamilton F. Disston, son of Philadelphia manufacturer Henry Disston. Henry's seven-story cottage is on the left side of the picture.

Popular restaurants were not limited to the elegant hotels. Sid Hartfield's, Captain Starn's, Abe's Oyster House, the Knife and Fork Inn, and Kent's helped make Atlantic City a mecca of culinary delights. Because of its location along the coast, seafood was, of course, a big draw. In 1897, Harry Dougherty opened Dock's Oyster House, a 60-seat seafood eatery on Atlantic Avenue. The family still operates Dock's, although the actual address on Atlantic Avenue has changed.

Not all the seafood was sold at restaurants like Dock's. Crab and beer joints like the one pictured here sprouted up along the boardwalk, especially near the Inlet.

Knife and Fork Inn, Atlantic City, N. J.

218895

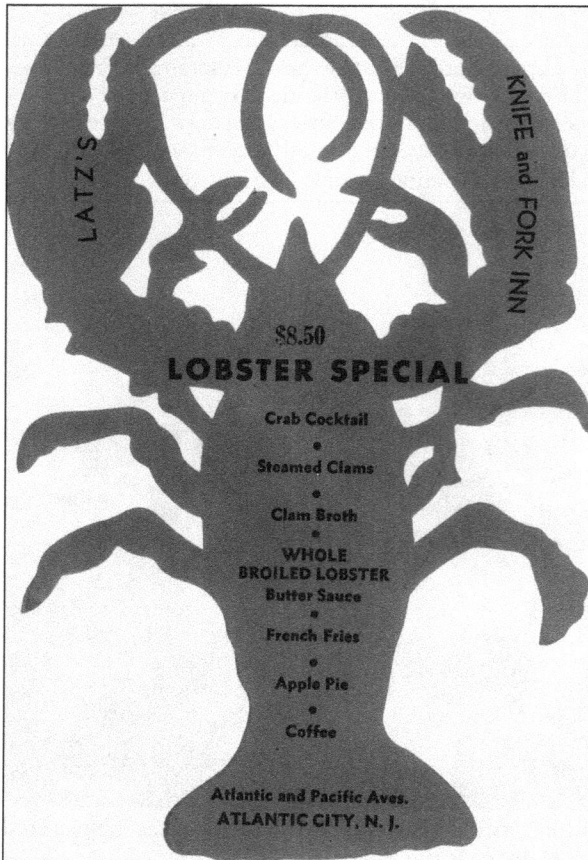

LATZ'S

KNIFE and FORK INN

$8.50
LOBSTER SPECIAL

Crab Cocktail
•
Steamed Clams
•
Clam Broth
•
WHOLE
BROILED LOBSTER
Butter Sauce
•
French Fries
•
Apple Pie
•
Coffee

Atlantic and Pacific Aves.
ATLANTIC CITY, N. J.

The Knife and Fork Inn, with its distinctive four-story Flemish structure shown above, was built in 1912 as an exclusive men's club. The second image features a menu in the shape of a lobster. During Prohibition, club members at the Knife and Fork defied the laws and openly served liquor at the bar, a practice prevalent in Atlantic City at the time. Not surprisingly, federal agents raided it. After the raid, membership declined. In 1927, the Latz family bought it, removed the bar, and converted the Knife and Fork into a restaurant. When Milton Latz passed in 1948, his sons Mack and Jim took over, with a clientele that included Frank Sinatra and Burt Lancaster. The two brothers could not get along, and in 1985, Mack bought out his brother. The aging Mack was unable to find a buyer and closed the Knife and Fork in 1997. Two years later, Mack's son Andrew leased the building until the Dougherty family, of Dock's Oyster House, purchased it in 2005.

Alexander Boardman came up with the country's first boardwalk, not as a place to stroll and shop, but as a necessity to prevent beachgoers from tracking sand into the lobbies of hotels. The original boardwalk in 1870 consisted of wooden planks laid on the sand each summer and removed when the season ended. The size and style of the boardwalk grew several times. By 1890, it was a permanent structure raised 10 feet off the ground with rails on each side, measuring 24 feet in width. A wider, longer boardwalk debuted in 1896. The boardwalk not only became the front street of hotels, stores, and other buildings, but a fashionable place to stroll—and still keep sand from the hotel lobbies. This photograph from the early 1900s features the Brighton Casino, built in 1894 as a modernized extension of the Brighton Hotel.

This 1915 picture shows the boardwalk teeming with strollers. It became one of Atlantic City's main attractions, as Champs-Elysées is to Paris, or Times Square is to New York City. In the background, a Ferris wheel speaks to joyous thrills. In the foreground, a stand sells artwork, while another pitches that unique Atlantic City treat: saltwater taffy. Legend credits David Bradley with the invention of the chewy confection when an 1883 northeaster soaked his candy stock; whether the story is true or not is open to debate. Joseph Fralinger entered the taffy business in 1885 and was soon joined by rivals from the Midwest, Enoch, Harry, and Lee James, who founded the James Candy Company. The two companies competed for customers' affections though the manufacturing process was similar. Taffy is first cooked in copper kettles over open coal fires, cooled on marble slabs, and pulled on a large hook on the wall. Pulling taffy is designed to add air to the corn syrup and sugar confection. By draping 10 to 25 pounds of cooled taffy over the hook and then pulling away from the hook, the taffy stretches. Fralinger's and James, now one company, continues to make taffy in Atlantic City and distributes it all over the country.

While hotels and stores went up on the landward side of the boardwalk, a new attraction grew on the ocean side. The amusement pier jutted hundreds of feet into the ocean and offered all manner of entertainment, passive and active. Howard's Pier, shown here, opened in 1882 at Kentucky Avenue as the first of its kind. Built by Col. George Howard and extending 650 feet, it offered theater, vaudeville, and concerts. A storm destroyed it, but a second one opened a year later, 856 feet long. In early 1884, a ship crashed into the structure, wrecking a portion of it. Howard's Pier was rebuilt again, in time for that summer. This incarnation lasted until the city purchased it to enlarge the boardwalk in 1889. By then, other piers, like Applegate Pier and Iron Pier, were in business. More followed before the century ended. Atlantic City would boast the most amusement piers of any coastal city in the world.

Capt. John L. Young, already successful with Young's Pier, launched Million Dollar Pier in July 1906, at Arkansas Avenue. The pier included vaudeville shows, an aquarium, and deep-sea net hauls. Captain Young also built a palatial three-story Venetian mansion with the address of 1 Atlantic Ocean in 1908. The photograph above shows workers building other parts of the pier adjacent to the house. The other image is a postcard of the residence, which featured marble statuary in the formal garden. This was not Captain Young's first pier home. He also built a cottage on Young and McShay's Pier, his first venture, 1,700 feet from the boardwalk, and outside of state control at the time.

These two photographs depict the interior of 1 Atlantic Ocean. Both images feature a sitting room within the mansion. In one room, Captain Young used wicker chairs in the photograph above; note the dining room in the background. In the photograph below, the decor shifts towards oversize chairs with a seashell motif. The arms and legs are designed like sea serpents and other aquatic creatures. Captain Young had the furniture in his villa custom made in Venice and imported the crystal chandeliers from Austria. He covered some of the walls with a moth and butterfly collection. Thomas Edison worked out the pastel lighting, inside and outside of the house.

President William H. Ta[ft]
at luncheon
Capt. Youngs Cottage
C. E. Convention
Atlantic City ~ July 19

© H. B. Smith.

More than Capt. John L. Young's family was entertained at 1 Atlantic Ocean. In July 1911, Pres. William H. Taft held court at a luncheon in the mansion for a few friends and associates, including a soldier. Taft was in Atlantic City to address the Christian Endeavor Convention, which brought together members of evangelical Protestant churches.

Iron Pier opened at Massachusetts Avenue in 1886. Named for its iron pilings, the pier had a large theater at one end. While the pier provided top stage shows, it could not compete, and in 1898, H. J. Heinz Company bought the pier, enlarged it to 1,000 feet, and used it as an exhibition hall for its 57 Varieties. Visitors could sample all 57. The company also offered writing rooms with free stationary and cooking demonstrations.

Garden Pier opened in 1913 near New Jersey Avenue. This photograph shows a central courtyard surrounded by buildings. In the background stands the B. F. Keith's Theatre. The Spanish Renaissance architecture and the beautifully landscaped gardens gave it a formal appearance that attracted an upscale crowd and gave the pier its name. The pier changed hands several times, and in 1918, it was known as B. F. Keith's Theatre and Palace of Dancing.

Bathhouse owner George Jackson opened Steel Pier in 1898 at Virginia Avenue. It took its name from the iron pilings and steel girders, which supported the structure. Over the years, the pier changed owners and size, eventually reaching 1,780 feet in length. It evolved into perhaps the most famous of the piers, presenting movies, concerts, stage shows, and the high diving horse.

Atlantic City offered the latest gadgets and attractions, large and small. This included one of the first roller coasters, which would be scary even by today's standard. The Loop the Loop on Young's Pier at Tennessee Avenue sent riders on a thrill loop. The ride opened in 1902 and was also known as the Flip Flap Railway. Although many passengers complained of neck and back injuries, the coaster lasted 10 years on Young's Pier, which was first dubbed Young and McShay's Pier, after Capt. John L. Young and Stewart McShay purchased Applegate Pier in 1891. The Loop the Loop has its place in Atlantic City amusement ride lore. So did others. In the 1890s, Atlantic City featured an illusory ride called the Haunted Swing. The resort also housed the first wheel ride. It debuted in Atlantic City in the early 1890s, created by William Somers, some two years before George Ferris unveiled his version for an exposition in Chicago. Somers filed a lawsuit over patent infringement, but Ferris died before the issue was settled, and in the end, the Ferris wheel stepped into history.

The piers were not just places to dance and party, see the latest entertainers of the day, eat junk food, or marvel at the latest modern science had to offer. They were also a place to sit a spell, particularly in the early years. These images show women and men relaxing in the salt air on pier pavilions over the ocean. They would read, write, or simply pass the time away doing nothing. The H. J. Heinz Company offered writing rooms and stationary, and Steel Pier had separate smoking and reading rooms. Fishing decks were popular as well.

By the 20th century, Atlantic City had become more than a beach and boardwalk with hotels and restaurants. It was a city, with residents and workers. The population exceeded 27,000. This image shows a busy intersection at Georgia and Arctic Avenues crowded with farmer's markets, huckster trucks, and other signs of commerce for a budding city. Pushcarts and horse-drawn carriages laden with fruits and vegetables gathered on almost every corner. While horses were still the main means of transport, note the early automobiles on the street. Houses and storefronts paint a picture of a busy neighborhood.

Two

ALL GROWN UP
1921–1945

The period began with the creation of the pageant that would become the Miss America, the matriarch of such events and the standard by which all others are still measured. The era ended with the close of World War II and the return of Atlantic City to civilians, after its role for the war efforts. In between, the resort flourished with new hotels and the expansion of existing ones to create a boardwalk lined with grand buildings such as the Ambassador, the Traymore, Haddon Hall, and the Breakers. This era saw the construction of the convention hall, an architectural marvel in its day and a national historic landmark now. Within the bowels of the hall lies the world's largest pipe organ. This period also led to the creation of one of the country's most popular and enduring board games, Monopoly, which is based in Atlantic City. Steel Pier evolved to win the title of Showplace of the Nation for its roster of stars. Nightspots such as Club Harlem emerged, and Atlantic City flaunted Prohibition and a ban on gambling.

Local business owners and hoteliers dreamed up the Miss America Pageant as an excuse to extend the traditional summer season a week beyond Labor Day. It began in 1921 with the creation of the Atlantic City Fall Pageant and its highlight, the Inter-City Beauty Contest. A total of eight young women competed, representing cities from Washington to New York and Atlantic City to Pittsburgh. Margaret Gorman, a 16-year-old from Washington, D.C., won the Golden Mermaid trophy that year, in a contest staged at the B. F. Keith's Theatre on Garden Pier. They crowned her, wrapped her in an American flag, and paraded her around as Miss America. She is seen here with Hudson Maxim, the inventor of smokeless gunpowder, who played King Neptune, a fixture at the pageant for many years. The inaugural proved such a success that 58 contestants strutted their stuff in 1922, including Gorman again. That year, the title went to Mary Campbell of Columbus, Ohio. Judges included Norman Rockwell, Lee Shubert, and Flo Ziegfeld, establishing the precedent of having celebrities pass judgment. Campbell went on to win again in 1923, becoming the only two-time Miss America winner.

Ruth Malcomson of Philadelphia won the Miss America title in 1924. At 17, she had won the amateur division in the 1923 Bather's Revue. A year later, she returned as Miss Philadelphia to face off against the largest field in the history of the pageant—84 representatives. She narrowly defeated returning champion Campbell. Malcomson decided not to defend her title due to her belief that professionals were entering what was still the Inter-City Beauty Contest, as a Hollywood film was to be shot around the 1925 pageant. Her decision drew controversy in the press and began false speculation that the contest was fixed. The pageant committee reacted quickly, by instituting a new rule that no Miss America could return to competition. The following year, Fay Lanphier of Oakland, California, won the title. Upon victory, she was whisked to New York City to appear opposite Louise Brooks and Douglas Fairbanks Jr. in Paramount's *The American Venus*, a thinly veiled film on the pageant.

One of the highlights of the annual pageant was the Miss America parade down the boardwalk. Above, a contestant rides in a seashell float as onlookers watch, often in rolling chairs. People sat rows deep to catch the parade, which has a longer history than the pageant itself. The first Floral Parade dated to the summer of 1902, when flower-decorated rolling chairs, each with a pretty girl, made its way down the boardwalk. Then in September 1920, the city held what was billed as the International Rolling Chair Parade, part of a fall pageant. Girls sat in chairs or on floats that paraded down the boardwalk. The rolling chairs continued to carry women throughout the 1920s.

In 1879, the three-story Haddon Hall Hotel, owned by Samuel and Susanna Wheaton Hunt, opened across North Carolina Avenue from the Chalfonte, 11 years its senior. The Leeds and Lippincott families purchased Haddon Hall in 1890, with Sarah Leeds named manager. A decade later, Leeds's son bought the Chalfonte, which in 1904 became the first fire proof hotel in the city. Operating as the Chalfonte-Haddon Hall, the two hotels grew to 1,000 guest rooms by 1928. The Chalfonte-Haddon Hall was noted as one of the more elegant luxury lodgings of the day, even boasting a pair of squash courts for the well-to-do Philadelphians who could not bear leaving the game behind on a vacation. As this aerial photograph shows, the two hotels fronted a bustling mini-metropolis of smaller hotels, boardinghouses, rooming houses, and residences. In the 1940s, the hotel served as the site for a hospital for wounded soldiers. In the late 1970s, it housed the first legal casino in the city.

25 THE TRAYMORE HOTEL, ATLANTIC CITY, N. J.

H. BECHER

The Traymore lorded over crowded beaches on summer days. Like so many other imposing hotels in Atlantic City, the Traymore began life as a small cottage, built in 1879. Depicted on the left is the first tower. With a series of expansions and the imprint of famed architect William L. Price, the building was completed in 1915, with 600 guest rooms. The Traymore's expansive facade passed for art deco years before the rise of the style. It was considered the look of Atlantic City and solidified the reputation of Price, a disciple of Frank Furness. The interior featured a sea fantasy decor for the Submarine Grille and included a ballroom that accommodated 4,000. In its day, the Traymore entertained Presidents Wilson, Coolidge, and Roosevelt; it also entertained several vice-presidents, as well as scientists, explorers, physicians, financiers, authors, musicians, dramatic and operatic stars, and social leaders, from both the United States and abroad.

George F. Lee and Hamilton F. Disston owned a tract of land fronting the boardwalk adjacent to Indiana Avenue and Park Place. The area was dubbed Brighton Park in honor of Lee's hotel by the same name across the street. The park, deeded to the city as a public area in perpetuity, also fronted the Marlborough-Blenheim Hotel, another of those mergers. This image shows the park looking south at the Marlborough and the larger Blenheim hotels in the 1920s. In honor of the 50th anniversary of Edison's light bulb, General Electric erected the Fountain of Light in the center of Brighton Park. Jets threw water as high as 30 feet in the air, which was illuminated by 72 various color effects. Brighton Park occupies one of the most expensive pieces of real estate in the world: the boardwalk and Park Place. The fountain is still there, but the boardwalk end of the park now houses a Korean War Memorial.

The Blenheim, pictured here, was another design from William L. Price. It was constructed in 1906, the first of its kind to be built with reinforced concrete. The design used a Spanish-Moorish theme, with signature dome and chimneys. It was also considered the first hotel to feature a private bath in each room and offered hot-and-cold running salt water. The adjacent

Marlborough House was constructed four years earlier, also designed by Price. Named for the Prince of Wales's home, the hotel employed a Queen Anne–style design. The Blenheim was also placed on the National Register of Historic Places. Both hotels were built by Josiah White III and his son John.

Convention hall, officially
known as the Atlantic
City Auditorium, held
the distinction of being
the largest building in the
world without roof posts
or pillars when it opened
in May 1929. Its cavernous
reverse (or upside-down)
shaped roof was ahead of its
time, both on an acoustic
and a lighting front. Built
for $13.4 million, the
hall covered seven acres,
including the plaza on the
boardwalk. The building
measured 488 by 288 feet
and at its height rose 137
feet high. The auditorium
also had the largest stage
in the world, capable of
holding the Rolling Stones's
Steel Wheels tour in 1989.
Convention hall played host
to the armed services during
World War II, and the
Beatles and Pres. Lyndon
Johnson in 1964. From
1940 to 2005, it housed
the Miss America Pageant.
The hall still stands and
remains on the National
Register of Historic Places.

The convention hall, bordered by the boardwalk and Pacific Avenue, Mississippi and Georgia Avenues, was wedged between residential streets, as this image from 1932 shows. Trucks that brought in concert equipment, and displays for the trade shows had to squeeze into these streets to load and unload. Typical of many beach block streets, rooming houses, small hotels, and residences lined the sidewalks on the opposite side of the hall.

In its long history, the convention hall served as a site for all manner of conventions and trade shows, as well as entertainment and sporting events. It was capable of holding 40,000 people throughout the building. College and high school football games were played here as early as 1930, long before the advent of indoor stadiums.

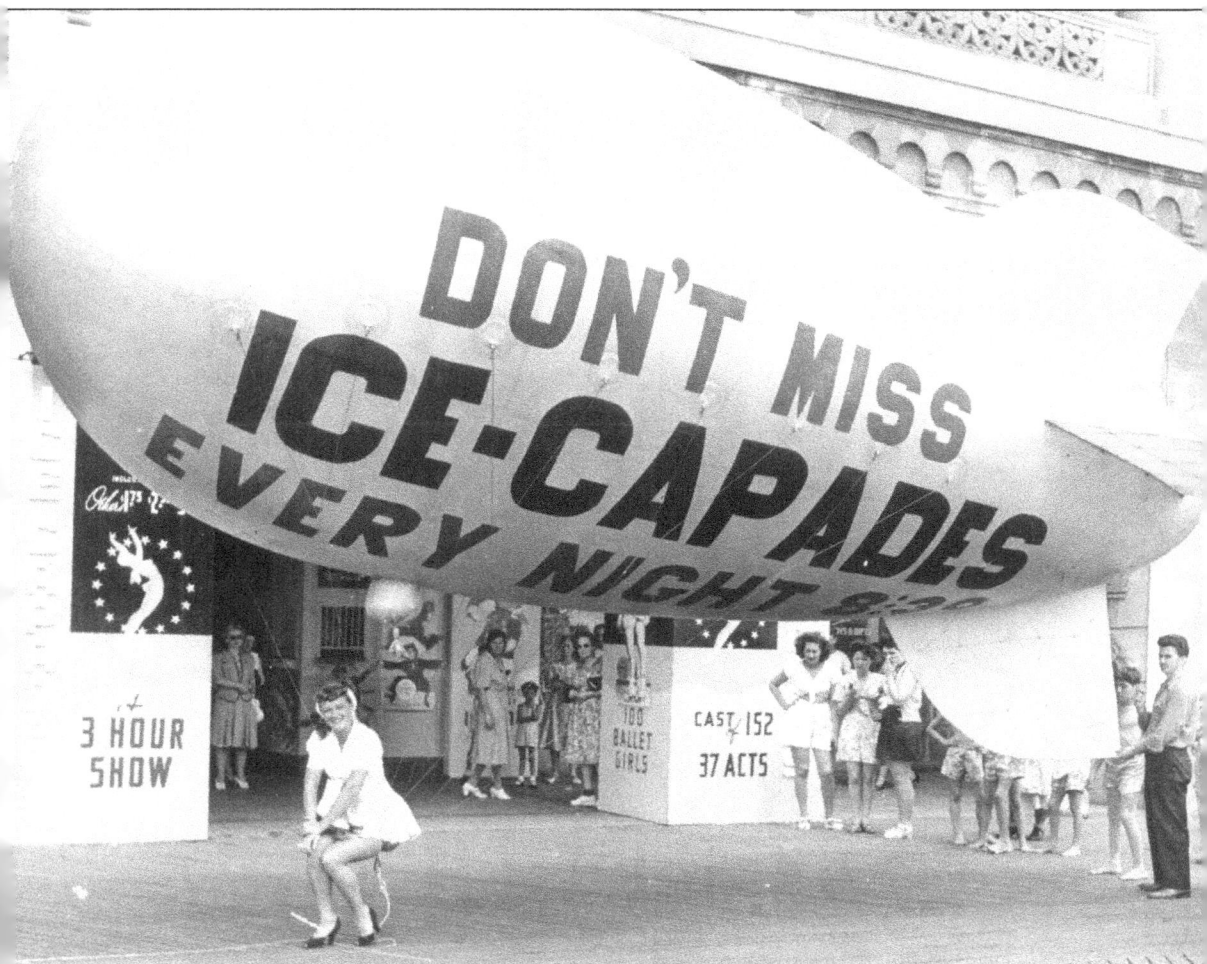

The Ice Capades was a constant fixture in the convention hall from 1941 through the 1980s. The popular ice show held its tryout runs at the hall every summer. This image shows a publicity balloon outside the hall with a performer in ice skates underneath. The convention hall also hosted a semiprofessional hockey team known as the Seagulls.

The convention hall houses the world's largest pipe organ. It was built between 1929 and 1932 to designs by Emerson L. Richards, an Atlantic City native and a state senator. Recognized by Guinness World Records as the biggest and loudest musical instrument, the exact number of pipes is unknown. The official figure is 33,114, but most organ experts peg the number at 32,000.

The beach was the place to see and be seen during Atlantic City's heyday. This 1930 image (above) shows the Marlborough-Blenheim, Dennis, and Shelburne Hotels in the background. Note the large crowds standing on the boardwalk, watching the throngs frolic and sunbathe on the beach. In the 1920s and 1930s, sand artists flourished, creating elaborate sculptures on the beach, sometimes three-dimensional and sometimes in relief. The artists often liked to work close to the boardwalk near the piers to reach more people who might be encouraged to contribute donations. Artists favored caricatures of news makers, famous paintings, and local themes like King Neptune.

Beach Scene Showing Sand Sculpture

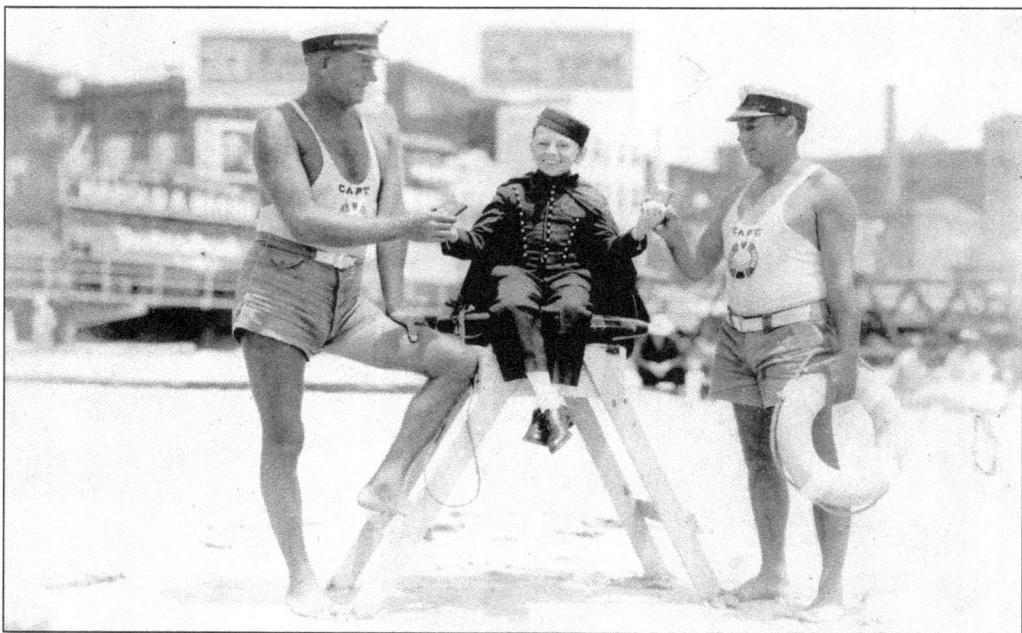

It was not just big name entertainers who caused a stir in Atlantic City. Above, lifeguard Capt. John "Rails" McCoullough (right) joins Capt. John Furlow in greeting Johnny, the "Call for Philip Morris" guy. In the picture below, lifeguards gather around the winner of the annual Miss Beach Patrol Pageant at the South Carolina Avenue headquarters in the early 1940s. The contest dates back to the 1920s and finally faded out in the 1970s. Lifeguards would approach women on the beach, soliciting applicants. During the contest, women donned bathing suits to be judged. The 10 finalists would come to the Lifeguard Ball in August, a dress up affair dating back to the 1890s. The ball was held at various hotels or nightspots such as the 500 Club, where Dean Martin crowned the winner one year.

Nighttime was always the bright time in Atlantic City. The city was a neon paradise that hawked entertainers and products such as cigarettes, paints, and soft drinks. The piers were a popular location for these signs because of their visibility over beach and ocean. They could be seen for miles, even out at sea. This 1931 image shows neon signage touting Coca-Cola. A number of the signs in Atlantic City were animated. For example, Sherwin Williams featured paint flowing over the globe.

This photograph, from 1941, highlights everything one would want to know about Steel Pier, from the Ink Spots and Gene Krupa to the *Dead End Kids* movie.

Several years after the Camden and Atlantic Railroad launched service, the rival Philadelphia and Atlantic City Railroad joined operations. Eventually, the Reading Railroad took over this line, while the Pennsylvania Railroad did the same with the Camden and Atlantic Railroad. Faced with shrinking profits during the Great Depression, the Pennsylvania and Reading Railroads in South Jersey merged in 1933, creating the Pennsylvania-Reading Seashore Lines. This image shows the new line's terminal.

Atlantic City hardware store operator William Hayday introduced rolling chairs in the 1880s to rent to the disabled on the boardwalk. He soon capitalized on their use for the able-bodied. Harry Shill, who manufactured the chairs, added two-and three-seat models to the mix. Over the years, the design has changed, but the wicker chair concept has remained. In this image, dozens of chairs roll by with Garden Pier and Heinz Pier in the background. The common man could experience royalty by being chauffeured through the crowds for all to see.

The boardwalk evolved into a major thoroughfare for commerce. This image shows the famed Planter's Peanut store, opened in 1930 across from Steel Pier on Virginia Avenue, one of the first retail outlets in the company. Mr. Peanut raises his top hat on the sign. The store kept its doors open so the aroma of the peanuts drifted across the boardwalk. A costumed version of Mr. Peanut became an icon on the boardwalk for years. The store closed in the 1970s.

Bring me your huddled masses yearning to stroll the boardwalk. Even when it was not in the heat of summer, crowds gathered on the famous wooden way, sharing space with the rolling chairs as this image shows in 1936. Central Pier can be seen in the background.

Steel Pier was a massive building compared to its neighbor, Steeplechase Pier. It earned its title as Showplace of the Nation for its variety of offerings for one low price. The ocean end of the pier housed water carnivals, including the famous high diving horse act. The boardwalk end housed a music hall, exhibits such as General Motors, and other attractions to entertain visitors.

This group portrait shows many of the employees and performers at the pier, including one of the diving horses. As the sign indicates, guests at the pier were able to choose among three movies, a minstrel show, and a vaudeville show. The pier's success in this era owes much to Frank P. Gravatt, who bought the attraction in 1925. It was Gravatt who pioneered the diverse entertainment options.

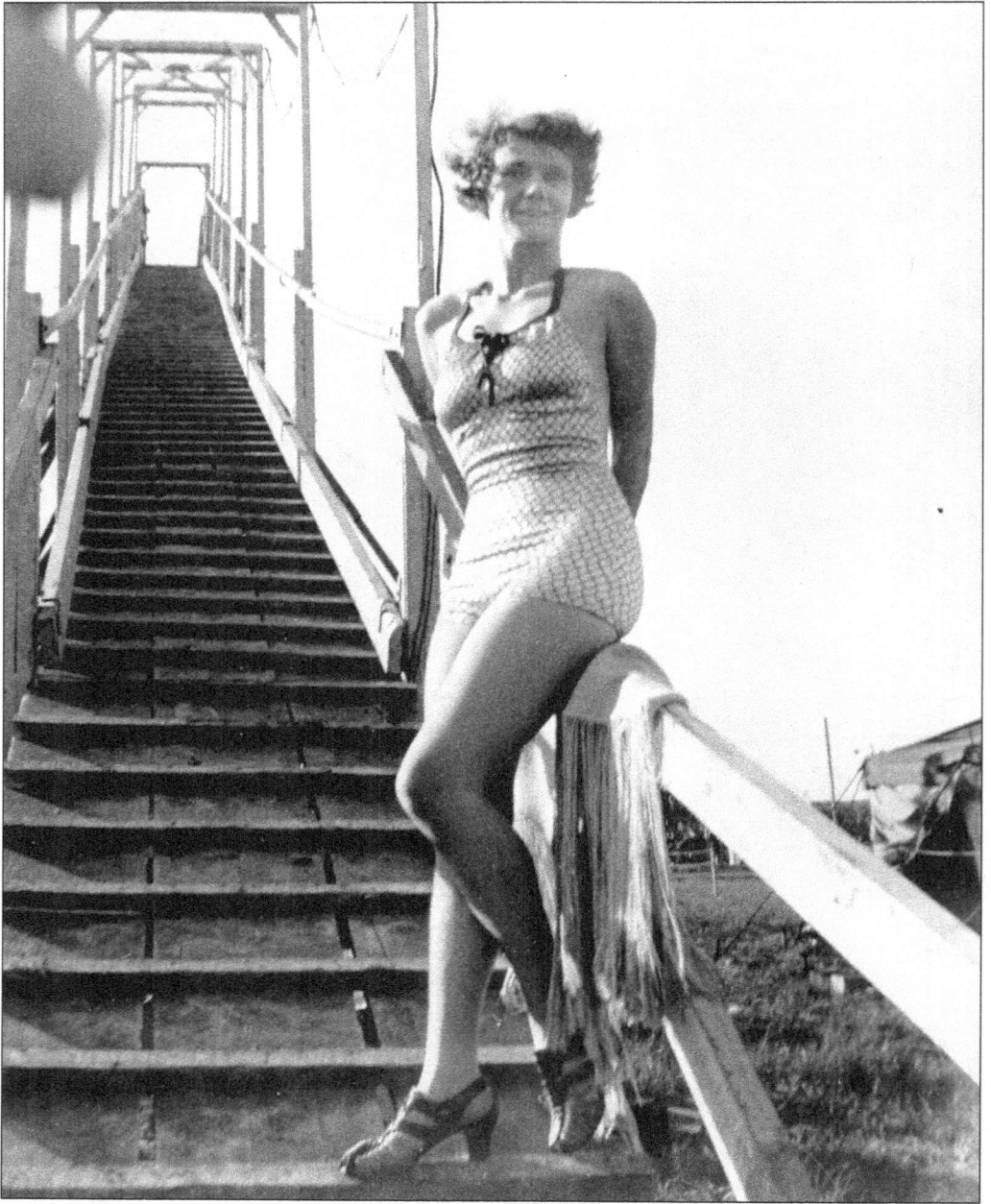

Arnette Webster French earned a reputation as a water performer, specializing in riding the high diving horses, a centerpiece at Steel Pier for years. In this photograph, French poses at the foot of the stairs leading to the ramp where she would climb aboard the horses for the leap.

Once aboard, the ramp would drop open and French and her horse dove into a tank of water. French's sister, Sonora Webster Carver, was the first woman to ride the diving horses on Steel Pier. Carver inspired the Disney movie *Wild Hearts Can't Be Broken*. Not to be undone, French appeared in the children's book *The Girl on the High-Diving Horse*.

Steel Pier's water show was more than the diving horse. It featured acrobatic water-skiers, even Rex the Wonder Dog, leading Arnette Webster French through the waves. Indeed, Steel Pier gave birth to show skiing in 1928 when entrepreneur Frank Sterling signed a contract to produce a water-sports show on a motorized device called a ski board. When the ski board proved ill suited for the water conditions, he switched to a new form of activity—waterskiing.

Pugilist felines like Professor Nelson's Boxing Cats, shown here, and aerial acrobatics joined the water performers and vaudevillians on Steel Pier. Kangaroos were made to stage fisticuffs as well. One had an exhibition match with heavyweight champion Primo Carnera.

Crowds gather inside the foyer, waiting for a chance to get into the Steel Pier music hall to catch Abbott and Costello or one of three photoplays on the bill. In later years, the music hall served as a stage for the best jazz and pop musicians and singers in the world, from Benny Goodman to Rick Nelson to the Rolling Stones. In the image below, Abbott and Costello relax on a rolling chair during one of their appearances in the city. The comic duo got their start doing minstrel shows on Steel Pier and elsewhere.

John Phillip Sousa and his band perform before a packed house in the ballroom of Steel Pier in this 1931 picture. Sousa was a frequent guest to many of the piers along the boardwalk. In 1903, he played free concerts at Steeplechase Pier. Sousa's love affair with the city had much to do with his wife, the daughter of a local photographer.

The reputation of Steel Pier attracted hordes of visitors hoping for admittance, as this 1930 picture attests. For a quarter, these folks were able to see movies, comics like Abbott and Costello, other entertainers, and the General Motors exhibit, which displayed the latest automotive products to vacationers. This tradition lasted decades.

Capt. John L. Young acquired his first pier at Tennessee Avenue. The former Applegate Pier was rechristened Young and McShay's Pier and later, after his partner Stewart McShay retired in 1897, Young's Ocean Pier. Captain Young lengthened it to 2,000 feet, and the pier featured vaudeville acts, dancing, and other entertainment. Dora Johnson introduced an African American strutting dance called the cakewalk. Captain Young built a small cottage for his family, an act he repeated in much grander style on Million Dollar Pier. Large billboards, like the one promoting Squibb's Dental Crème, dominated the pier as it did others in the city. Fire ravaged Young's Old Pier in 1912. The building remained in disrepair until a shorter version was rebuilt by a new company and named Central Pier. It housed offices and commercial exhibits like Texaco's Romance of Oil.

In this 1934 image, Capt. John L. Young shares a rolling chair with John Eveler, a chair operator. Captain Young, a former lifeguard, policeman, fisherman, and carpenter before turning entrepreneur, entered into the amusement business with Stewart McShay when they bought the Victoria Skating Rink on South Carolina Avenue in 1887. They built the Merry-Go-Round Casino and installed the largest carousel in the resort, equipped with an orchestrion organ and a library of almost 100 classical records. The building had a glass room on the ocean side that was heated in the winter.

When he bought the piers, Captain Young, a seafood lover, began the daily net hauls, which brought up fish and other creatures of the briny deep at the end of the piers, to the delight of paying visitors and onlookers. He would also fish off the piers from the comfort of his homes.

Like other piers, Garden Pier offered one-price admission. In this case, the price was 10¢. One could chip in another quarter to fish off the end of the pier. The Spanish Renaissance architecture of the buildings and the beautifully landscaped gardens gave the pier a formal appearance, which attracted an upscale crowd. The pier, opened in 1913, housed one of the city's largest ballrooms, where a young Rudolph Valentino worked as a dance instructor and large conventions met before the Atlantic City Auditorium was built in 1929. The image above shows the B. F. Keith's Theatre in the background. The image below includes a view of the Breakers Hotel on New Jersey Avenue.

The centerpiece of Garden Pier was the stately B. F. Keith's Theatre, which for many years rivaled any of those on Broadway. *Tobacco Road* and *George White's Scandals* premiered there. This theater, named after famed vaudeville producer B. F. Keith, also hosted the first Miss America Pageant in 1921. Still, the theater, like the pier itself, struggled to stay afloat financially, in part because of its uptown location.

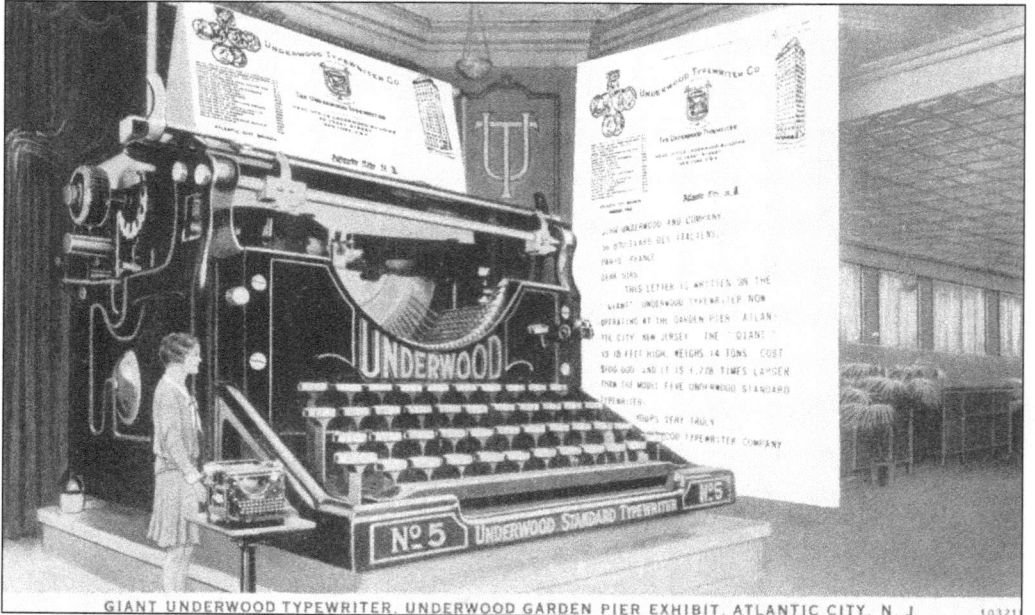

GIANT UNDERWOOD TYPEWRITER. UNDERWOOD GARDEN PIER EXHIBIT, ATLANTIC CITY, N. J.   10321

Piers did more than entertain; they also brought in corporate advertisers. Steel Pier featured a General Motors exhibit for years, and a Ford exhibit before that. Central Pier touted its Texaco exhibition. Garden Pier had a huge, larger-than-life Underwood typewriter. It stood 18 feet high and weighed 14 tons. Note the large letter actually typed with the typewriter.

In 1938, showman George Hamid took over Million Dollar Pier and renamed it Hamid's Million Dollar Pier or, simply, Hamid's Pier. In addition to retaining Capt. John L. Young's fishing hauls, the pier under Hamid also had an aquarium and sundeck, with nightly dancing. Like Steel Pier, which Hamid bought in 1945, Million Dollar Pier offered films and stage shows, with entertainers such as Paul Whiteman, George Jessel, and the Three Del Rios siblings, dwarf performers Trinidad, Delores, and Paul Rodriguez.

As with the other piers in the resort, neon signs and other advertising billboards were an important part of the Million Dollar Pier ambience. This view looking south highlights the Sherwin Williams Paint Company sign, which at night showed the colors flowing down the globe in neon. Seagram's advertised for its liquor products and Philip Morris touted its cigarettes.

No one would confuse Atlantic City with the Wild West. But the Dude Ranch, owned by Tom Endicott, was a western-styled nightclub and restaurant at Connecticut Avenue and the boardwalk. Guests entered by walking through the bowed legs of a 30-foot cowboy that framed the doorway into the club. The Dude Ranch was built on the site of an old carousel, so it had a round dance floor.

The first jitneys debuted in 1915, little more than a large automobile. The name came from an old English term for a nickel, which happened to be the fare. With no regulations in place, the number of jitneys exploded to almost 500. In 1916, the city set routes and established the fare. It later limited the number to 190. Sedan-style jitneys, like the one shown here in the early 1940s, remained the norm until 1947.

African Americans were as much a part of the Atlantic City history as the well-to-do Philadelphians from the Main Line who frequented the fashionable hotels. The city developed a large population, many who worked as low-paid service workers—maids, cooks, and doormen, for example—which catered to the tourists. But the black population lived north of Arctic Avenue, in a type of de facto segregation. African Americans were kept off the boardwalk and away from most of the beaches. The boisterous or improperly dressed were kept out of theaters and hotel lobbies. Still, their communities flourished. In this image, a fraternal organization poses for a picture on Arctic Avenue by an old hotel and boardinghouse.

John Henry "Pop" Lloyd was a folk hero in Atlantic City. He played for the Bacharach Giants, an Atlantic City baseball team in one of the Negro Leagues. He played for them in 1922, 1924, and 1925, and again in 1931 and 1932. A line-drive hitter whose skills at shortstop drew favorable comparisons to Honus Wagner, Lloyd was one of the best black players of the dead-ball era. He was known for his aggressive, fearless base running. His great range and large, steady hands led Cuban fans to dub him "El Cuchara" or "the Shovel." He once caught a game while wearing a wire wastepaper basket to protect his face because his team could not afford to buy a catcher's mask. Lloyd later became a player-manager and was given the affectionate nickname "Pop" by the young players. A stadium in Atlantic City bears his name. The National Baseball Hall of Fame's Negro Leagues Committee elected Lloyd to the hall in 1977, 12 years after his passing in Atlantic City.

African Americans did more than work in the hotels. They also entertained, especially on a stretch of Kentucky Avenue between Arctic and Atlantic Avenues, known for its rib joints and hot clubs. The focal piece of Kentucky Avenue was Club Harlem, the legendary 900-seat club that opened in 1932. The best black performers in the country appeared at one time or another, from Sammy Davis Jr. and Billy Eckstine to Duke Ellington and Count Basie, and later Jackie Wilson, Sarah Vaughn, and Ray Charles. Come Sunday morning, celebrities and others gathered for the 6:00 a.m. breakfast show. Larry Steele, shown here, was a fixture at Club Harlem, home to Steele's "Smart Affairs" show, which featured a chorus line known as the Beige Beauties. Steele's emceeing set the pace for an audience that never clapped their hands. When they arrived at their table, there were knockers, long sticks with a round ball of painted wood on the end, that the patrons used to knock on the wooden tables to show their appreciation for the acts.

Atlantic City attracted celebrities from the world of entertainment. The city jump-started the careers of John Philip Sousa, W. C. Fields, Paul Whiteman, Abbott and Costello, and Dean Martin and Jerry Lewis. Marlena Deitrich, posing in a rolling chair in this image, appears at a war bond rally in the early 1940s.

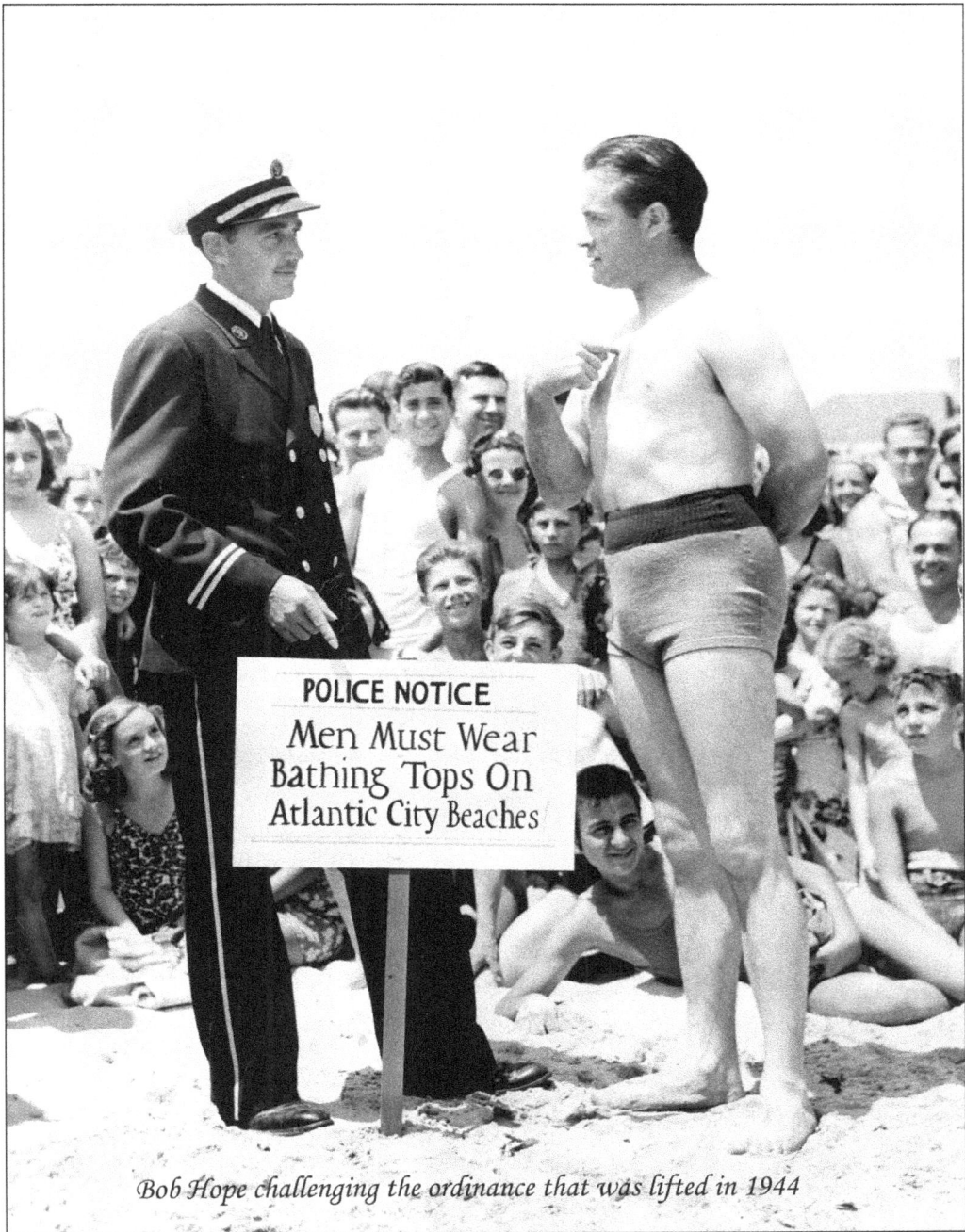

Bob Hope challenging the ordinance that was lifted in 1944

Bob Hope played Steel Pier and was also an original stockholder at Atlantic City Race Course. His monologues were full of political quips and barbs, so it comes as no surprise that Hope would mug topless with a local law enforcement officer, protesting a long-standing ordinance requiring men to wear tops. By 1928, women were allowed to bathe without stockings, but men were not allowed to swim shirtless until the 1940s.

Atlantic City, whose year-round population never exceeded 70,000, boasted more than two dozen movie theaters during this era, not counting those on the amusement piers. The first ones on the boardwalk included the Savoy, the Alhambra, and the Victoria. The Bijou opened even earlier, in 1903, on Atlantic Avenue. By the 1920s, palatial movie houses dotted the city. One of the grandest of these was the Warner, near Arkansas Avenue. Harry M. Warner dedicated the theater in 1929 and star-studded world premieres were soon frequent occurrences. The Strand opened in 1910 as the Criterion. The above image of the Strand in 1936 shows the Clark Gable picture *San Francisco* on the marquee. The Virginia Theater is showing *Kept Husbands* in the 1931 picture on the left.

Atlantic City was not just a vacation haven. By the 1930s, more than 66,000 lived in the resort. Families took root in Atlantic City, and schools became necessary. A typical small-town high school was opened in 1923, across Albany Avenue from spacious Chelsea Park, and less than a block from the beach and boardwalk. It was built to hold 2,100 students. The school had its own pipe organ, adding to the city's reputation for huge organs. Neighboring towns of Brigantine, Ventnor, Margate, and Longport all sent their students to Atlantic City High. Newscaster Jessica Savitch and actress Phyllis Newman were among the graduates from the school. A new high school opened its doors in the mid-1990s, following an investment of more than $83 million.

A devastating hurricane ripped through Atlantic City on September 14, 1944. The storm traveled at speeds of 35 miles per hour and arrived at high tide. Many vacationers cancelled their reservations. While it lasted only a couple of hours, damages exceeded $4.5 million. Streets in the city's Inlet section filled with more than three feet of water. The storm destroyed half the boardwalk. The boardwalks in neighboring Ventnor, Margate, and Longport also sustained heavy damage as winds reached 85 miles per hour. This hurricane spelled the end of Heinz Pier, as these images show. Note the missing 5 blown away by the winds. No hurricane since has had that kind of impact.

During World War II, the United States Army commandeered Atlantic City, the only town in the continental United States that was transformed into a military base. From May 1942 to January 1946, the resort, dubbed Camp Boardwalk, hosted more than 400,000 servicemen and women, first as a basic training post for Army Air Corps and Coast Guard recruits, then as a redistribution center for returning airmen. The posh hotels along the boardwalk became military barracks, stripped of their plush carpets, fancy drapes, and comfortable bedding. The Army Air Force used the convention hall for administrative offices, and for troop training and briefings. The Chalfonte-Haddon Hall Hotel became the Thomas M. England General Hospital, the largest of its kind in the country. All types of surgery were performed, including amputations. The 1944 hurricane forced the evacuation of patients, who were carried down fire escapes and transported to a smaller hospital on Staten Island.

Troops did calisthenics on the beach. At times, they exercised inside the convention hall. Soldiers practiced beachfront landings while onlookers watched, as the image below shows. Machine-gun turrets were manned atop the hotels in case of attack. At night, the lamps on the boardwalk were shaded to ward off attacks by German U-boats, rumored to be patrolling the New Jersey coast. The resort continued to function as best it could. Entertainers like Tommy Dorsey and Harry James played the piers; soldiers received cut-rate prices at local movie theaters; local girls—even some Miss America contestants—volunteered to serve as dance partners.

Three

OLD AGE SETS IN
1946–1963

With the war over, Atlantic City tried to resume its place as the premiere vacation destination in the United States. But ominous rumblings were heard from afar, as air travel became more convenient and more affordable. Bugsy Seigel kicked off the evolution of Las Vegas with the opening of the Flamingo. Florida became a popular destination, as did California and Disneyland. Atlantic City did not seem as exotic as it used to be. As the 1950s gave way to the 1960s, the old dowagers on the boardwalk showed their age. With declining revenue, owners failed to keep up with renovations and the deterioration accelerated. Still, the city motored on. The 500 Club paired an unknown singer with an unknown comic and history was made, with the launch of Dean Martin and Jerry Lewis. Steel Pier and Club Harlem continued to showcase stars.

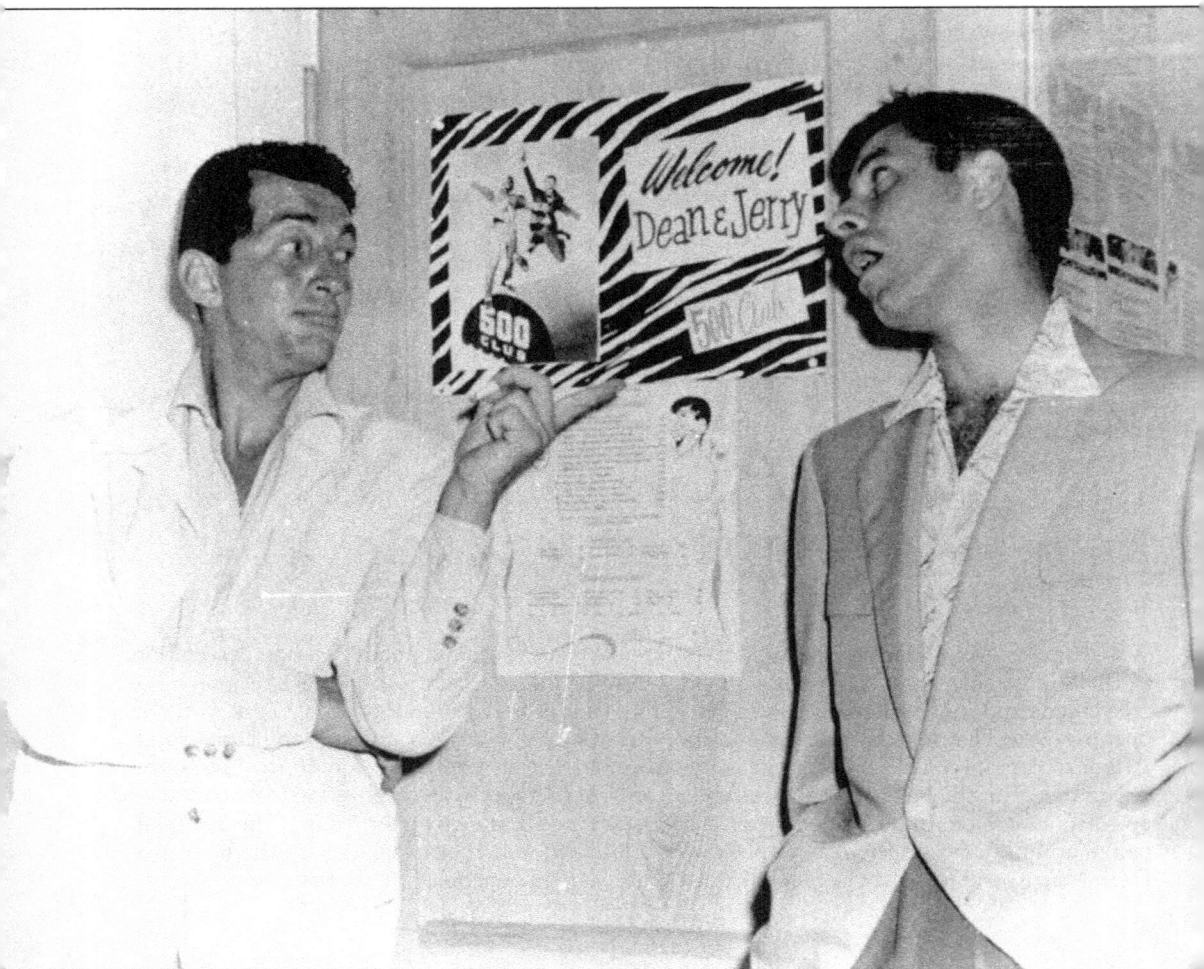

In 1946, two struggling entertainers, Jerry Lewis and Dean Martin, were slated to appear at the 500 Club at the same time. Stories vary whether the fortuitous coupling was staged or happenstance, but when Lewis took the stage during Martin's act, fireworks ensued and one of the most popular duos was born. According to Lewis's camp, one of the other entertainers at the club quit. Lewis, who had worked with Martin at the Glass Hat in New York City, suggested Martin as a replacement. At first they worked separately, but then ad-libbed together, improvised insults and jokes, squirted seltzer water, hurled bunches of celery, and exuded general zaniness. In less than 18 weeks, their salaries soared from $250 a week to $5,000. Martin had a slightly different story, according to some, saying that Lewis had nothing to do with the billing.

Martin and Lewis clown it up at the 500 Club in this photograph. As a result of their pairing on July 25, 1946, the two went on to a 10-year career making movies and returning to the club that made them famous. During that time, they made 16 films together.

Here Martin and Lewis flank 500 Club owner Paul "Skinny" D'Amato. The Five, as it was called, was the Atlantic City home of Frank Sinatra, but was also considered a hangout for the mob and local politicos. It was built by a Philadelphia mobster who tapped D'Amato to manage the club, at 6 South Missouri Avenue. A fire in 1973 ended the 500 Club's storied history.

The war ended, and Atlantic City returned to normal. Instead of soldiers exercising on the beach and marching on the boardwalk, the typical visitor took control. In this early spring image, strollers peruse the stores on the boardwalk, shopping and enjoying the weather. The still-thriving Steel Pier advertises Jimmy Dorsey and Lee Castle.

Large nighttime crowds gathers in front of the Planter's Peanut store at Virginia Avenue, still a fixture on the boardwalk across from Steel Pier. But change hung in the air. The Glaser family took over the James Candy Company in 1947, and by 1949, a Howard Johnson's restaurant had opened up next to Planter's.

MILLION DOLLAR PIER, ATLANTIC CITY, N. J.—29

Midway down the boardwalk, Million Dollar Pier still drew crowds as well. The ballroom attracted dancers, weary of the war and looking for a good time. The Miss America Pageant returned to the convention hall after a few years at the Warner Theater, when the military took over the hall for its use. In 1948, George Hamid gave the pier back to the sons of the former owners, Clarence and Filbert Crossan.

BALLROOM, HAMID'S MILLION DOLLAR PIER, ATLANTIC CITY, N. J.—91.

A fire ravaged Million Dollar Pier on September 13, 1949. The ballroom and some concessions were destroyed in the blaze, which left half of the pier and 41 rolling chairs as charred wreckage. Damage was estimated to be close to $200,000, which was high for that time. It was one of a number of fires that consumed boardwalk businesses through the years.

The pier underwent a change in the aftermath of the fire. The front end was converted into amusement rides and carnival games, which became the focal point on the pier through the 1950s and 1960s. Construction is seen here. The Shelburne Hotel is to the right.

Despite the changes swirling around the resort, the Atlantic City skyline still impressed when viewed from the ocean. The photograph above shows, from left to right, the Shelburne, Dennis, Marlborugh-Blenheim, Claridge, Traymore, and Chalfonte-Haddon Hall Hotels. The view below looks south with the Traymore in the foreground. The names of the hotels retained a magic ring to them. Posh monikers and exterior views from a distance, however, could not hide the slow deterioration going on in the inside, as vacancy rates climbed. Two-week stays, once common, gave way to weekend jaunts, and even day trips.

The Ambassador Hotel opened in 1919 and was among the larger hotels on the boardwalk. By 1950, the hotel already amassed a storied history, both famous and infamous. Operatic tenor Enrico Caruso sang in the Renaissance Salon in 1920. Pres. Warren Harding and Sir Arthur Conan Doyle vacationed there. Pres. Plutarco Elias Galles of Mexico was a guest, as were William Jennings Bryan and Baron Ago Von Maltzen, German ambassador to the United States. Samuel Gompers and people in the theatrical, motion picture, and sports worlds stayed there. And in May 1929, mob kingpins from around the country, including Meyer Lansky, Lucky Luciano, Dutch Schultz, and Al Capone, gathered for a three-day national convention to seek ways to end their bloody wars, coordinate national racketeering activities, and reign in Capone, whose ferocity unnerved even them.

Film siren Marilyn Monroe served as the grand marshal for the annual Miss America parade. Her presence spoke to the growing importance of the parade as part of the festivities surrounding a pageant already in the midst of change. The 1947 version marked the first time that contestants wore two-piece swimsuits in competition. Miss America entered the era of television in 1954 when the pageant sold the rights to ABC for $10,000. More than 27 million tuned in to see Lee Ann Meriwether, Miss California, crowned Miss America. Grace Kelly served as a judge. Bert Parks came on board as emcee the next year, which also marked the premiere of Bernie Wayne's song "There She Is."

This image shows Steeplechase Pier on a late July day in 1957. Located at Pennsylvania Avenue and the boardwalk, the pier opened in 1899 as the Auditorium Pier. George C. Tilyou bought it in 1902 and for a couple of years continued to bring in theater and performers like John Philip Sousa to the auditorium that gave it the original name. But the pier failed to draw enough, so in 1904, Tilyou remodeled it similar to his Coney Island Steeplechase Park and renamed it Steeplechase Pier. Visitors walked through the mouth of a large clown to enter. Tourists could rent clown costumes to wear on rides such as the Whirlpool and Whip. Other rides included the Sugar Bowl Slide, the Mexican Hat Bowl, and the Flying Chairs, which swung riders out over the ocean. Fire destroyed the pier in 1932, and it was later rebuilt without the clown face, but still with rides.

In the off-season, visitors could still ride horses on the beach, a practice that lasted through the 1960s. An ordinance approved in 1905 banned horses on the beach between June 1 and October 1. Another banned them altogether in the late 1980s. However, horseback riding was recently resurrected on the beach, from late fall to early spring.

Chicken Bone Beach, at Missouri Avenue, was the bathing spot for African Americans as much due to social restrictions as preference on the part of the community. Here a group poses on the beach in the 1950s. Thousands of vacationing African American families flocked to the shore with their chicken-laden picnic hampers, hence the name Chicken Bone Beach. It was more than regular families who sunbathed here, however. The beach attracted black entertainers such as Sammy Davis Jr., Louis Jordan, the Mills Brothers, Moms Mabley, and Club Harlem showgirls. In the picture to the right, rising basketball star Wilt Chamberlain (left), from Philadelphia, greets Ruppert Chase, a local African American Republican leader.

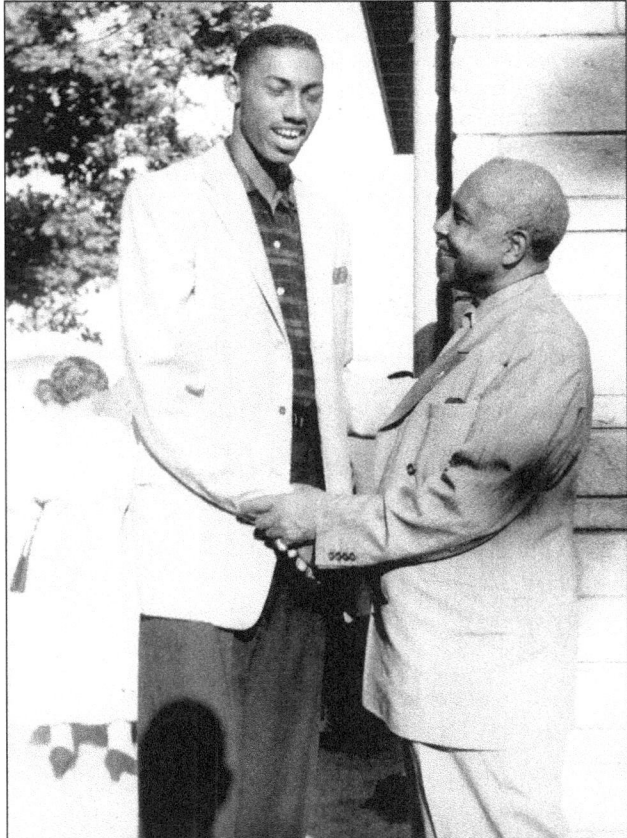

Despite the declining vacancy rates at the hotels, the boardwalk still drew crowds, as these images from winter in the early 1960s show. An array of nationwide chains like McCrory's, mixed with local favorites such as Kohr Brothers and James Salt Water Taffy, still drew visitors. One image includes a billboard for the game of Skilo. In a thinly veiled case of deception, Skilo and other five-letter games were Atlantic City's work-around for a prohibition on bingo. A little farther south is Taylor's Pork Roll, another popular eatery in Atlantic City, and the famed Sid Hartfield's restaurant, as well as Teepee Town, a toy store with a western motif.

Transportation changed as the 1950s approached. By the late 1940s, chairs operated by electric motors joined the traditional rolling chairs, carting visitors up and down the boardwalk. In the above image, an electric rolling chair approaches the Planter's Peanut store near Virginia Avenue and Fralinger's, a saltwater taffy shop and a fixture on the boardwalk since the mid-1880s.

This image features a coach-styled jitney making a stop on Pacific Avenue. The last sedan jitney ended its run in 1950. The first of these mini-buses carried eight passengers and cost a dime. Eventually, the jitney would increase its passenger capacity to 13. Fares increased in 1951 to a quarter for two rides during the season.

The beach was still a reason to come to Atlantic City. Here beach patrol chief Richard W. Hughes, along with Meredith Kerstedder, commissioner of public safety, swear in the class of 1958. Hughes was the first chief to bring the beach patrol into the modern era, teaching resuscitation methods in the days before cardio pulmonary resuscitation was standard.

The Brighton Hotel in the late 1950s had its own pool in front of the building. Gone were the days when actress Lillian Russell made nice with "Diamond Jim" Brady, the railroad magnate known for wearing jeweled stickpins. The Claridge Hotel, just visible on the left, replaced the Disston cottage across from Brighton Park. The 20-story Claridge was the last of the grand hotels built in the resort when it opened in 1930.

Dean Martin and Jerry Lewis were not the only superstars to bring in the crowds at the 500 Club. Frank Sinatra became a fixture at Paul "Skinny" D'Amato's nightspot—and a good friend of D'Amato. Sinatra is shown here on stage with fellow rat packer and Philadelphia comic Joey Bishop on the left.

Richard Nixon shakes hands with Frank "Hap" Farley, the Republican boss of Atlantic City and a state senator. Some rumored that Farley was a strong-arm kingpin who controlled everything from the Atlantic City Police Department to county patronage jobs to judges. But he was also the driving force behind the construction of the Atlantic City Expressway, along with the Atlantic Community College, Richard Stockton College of New Jersey, the Farley State Marina, and the West Hall expansion of the convention hall.

Four

NAILS IN THE COFFIN
1964–1974

Atlantic City had a watershed year in 1964. The Beatles spent three days in town during their first tour of North America, playing at the convention hall to hordes of screaming girls that August. Politics, however, took center stage that year. A number of motels opened to accommodate the rush of visitors expected for the Democratic National Convention, held in the end of August that year. The Democrats, meeting for the first time since the assassination of John F. Kennedy, nominated Lyndon B. Johnson. Since the nomination was a foregone conclusion, the national press, in search of stories to write about, focused on Atlantic City itself. Their report was not friendly. The city received bad grades for service and accommodations. More than anything else, the convention ended Atlantic City's run as a resort. Conventions still came to town, and so did vacationers. The hotels and the skyline remained unchanged, Steel Pier limped along, the convention hall had its moments, and Miss America still reigned. The road was clear, however. Atlantic City was in trouble unless something dramatic was done—and that something was casino gambling. A referendum in 1974 asked voters to approve casino gaming in New Jersey. The voters spoke, and they said no.

The Democrats held their lovefest in the convention hall from August 24 to 27, with the spirit of John F. Kennedy—and his picture—never far away. Lyndon B. Johnson's friendship with New Jersey governor Richard J. Hughes is often credited as a major reason Atlantic City hosted the convention that year. Robert Kennedy gave an impassioned 22-minute speech on August 27, 1964, citing his brother John F. Kennedy and his agenda as a way to introduce a short film on him. The uninterrupted applause left Kennedy in tears before delivering his speech. He said, "So I join with you in realizing that what started four years ago—what everyone here started four years ago—that is to be sustained; that is to be continued. The same effort and the same energy and the same dedication that was given to President John F. Kennedy must be given to President Lyndon Johnson and Hubert Humphrey."

The top image shows a ticket for admission into the Democratic National Convention. For the most part, the events inside the hall lacked much drama beyond an occasional rousing speech. That did not mean there was no controversy. At the forefront of this controversy was the battle over the Mississippi delegation. Civil rights activist Fannie Lou Hamer headed Mississippi Freedom Democratic Party, which challenged the regular party's right to seat an all-white delegation. Supporters flocked to Atlantic City from all over the country. Hubert H. Humphrey, who got the nod to be Johnson's vice presidential nominee at the convention, brokered a compromise. Beyond that wrinkle, the convention had little contention, and the focus of reporters from the national press shifted to Atlantic City: its lack of attractions, hotels with bad plumbing, and even worse service.

The local community was in awe of the Democratic National Convention. Atlantic City's politicians took full advantage of the media attention and the high profile counterparts in their midst. In the photograph to the left, Mayor Richard Jackson meets Lyndon B. Johnson. In the image below, the mayor holds court with Hubert H. Humphrey, the vice presidential nominee. Jackson also met with Lady Bird Johnson and Linda Bird outside the Traymore Hotel. The poor publicity that would come had to wait for another day.

Three days after Johnson and the Democrats left town, another whirlwind blew in. The Beatles played convention hall on August 30. Impresario George Hamid planned to book the Fab Four onto his Steel Pier, but he feared a crush of teenagers could prove dangerous to the pier's floor over the sand and surf, so he switched to the more stable convention hall. The Liverpool lads spent a few days in Atlantic City, built around their concerts here and in Philadelphia. Instead of lodging at a large boardwalk hotel, the boys holed up at the Lafayette Motor Inn, shown here in the late 1940s. A block off the boardwalk on North Carolina, the Lafayette was considered a safe bet to keep the Beatles hidden from fans. It did not work, as throngs of teenagers surrounded the hotel. The boys had to be spirited in and out of the hotel through secret passages. That did not stop them from enjoying some of the local delicacies, like the huge hoagie from the White House Sub Shop. White House employee Bobby Palamaro posed with the Beatles for this picture above inside the hotel room.

In the image above, electric rolling chairs roll past the Marlborough-Blenheim. The first proposal for an electrified chair came in 1907, using storage batteries. The ordinance proposed to permit their use, but the bill was killed. An attempt in 1918 also failed. Success finally came in 1948, when a law permitted 100 electric rolling chairs. Pedal power on the boardwalk was also popular in the morning, and still is. In the 1960s, the Marlborough-Blenheim added motel wings (as shown in both images), conference rooms, and a new pool. Its owner, Josiah White IV, the grandson of the builder, saw the changes as a way to keep his hotel afloat. The future would prove him wrong.

The Atlantic City beach patrol has yielded two mayors of the city. Both are pictured here as part of a training session on the beach. On the left is James Whelan, who served as mayor for three terms, from 1990 to 2002. In the center is Robert Levy, who went on to become beach patrol chief, took over as mayor in 2006. On the right is Lt. Frances Bennett.

In 1970, the city dedicated the new West Hall addition to the convention hall. As part of the ceremony, a helicopter flew in the cavernous East Hall. The addition, between Georgia and Florida Avenues, expanded the amount of floor space in the hopes of attracting larger conventions; it did not work. The number of convention visitors dropped from 475,000 per year in 1970 to 225,000 in 1980.

The annual Miss America parade winds down the boardwalk past the convention hall. By the early 1970s, a new tradition began in the parade, in which contestants would raise their feet to reveal often-outlandish footwear to the chants of "show us your shoes" from onlookers. The idea started as a joke when drag queens, dressed like Miss America, were in balconies overlooking the boardwalk near New York Avenue. From this vantage point, they could see that the women wore slippers or went barefoot, so they began shouting, "show us your shoes." Playing along, the contestants raised their feet to reveal no shoes at all. After that, it was not much of a stretch to go from no shoes to wacky shoes. The decorations would often speak to the state the women represented; Miss Wisconsin would don cheese shoes and Miss Nevada put a pair of dice on her feet. The tradition proved an integral part of the parade experience.

Long before the Astrodome and similar domed stadiums, Atlantic City's convention hall hosted the first indoor football games. In 1930, Washington and Jefferson College defeated Lafayette 7-0. A year later, the Frankford Legion crushed the Atlantic City Olympics, 41-0, in an early professional game. The playing surface, in the earlier years, consisted of natural grass sod that was grown outside, and then moved indoors for the game. The Liberty Bowl was played here in 1964. These 1972 images show the Boardwalk Bowl, held in the hall between 1961 and 1973. From 1968 to 1972, it was the NCAA Division II Mideast championship game. In 1973, the last year for the bowl, it was the Division II national semifinal.

This image shows the demolition of the Breakers and St. Charles Hotels at New Jersey Avenue and the boardwalk on May 3, 1974. Two years earlier, the massive Traymore fell in mere seconds, after being blown up. Four years later, the Marlborough-Blenheim imploded despite efforts to save the Blenheim portion of the complex. Reese Palley, who owned the hotel in the late 1970s, succeeded in having the Blenheim placed on the National Register of Historic Places.

While the city crumbled, the Ice Capades still held its annual summer tune-up in the convention hall. This photograph shows the cast of the 1975 edition of the famed show in 1974. Alas, even the Ice Capades eventually called it quits in Atlantic City.

The Absecon Lighthouse was not immune to the deterioration of Atlantic City. Neglect, and its presence in a neighborhood heading for ruin, took its toll on the exterior, as shown here. The interior did not fare much better. Still, the lighthouse held its ground, waiting for a new tomorrow. It earned designation on the National Register of Historic Places in 1971. A year earlier, the lighthouse received a similar designation from New Jersey. A group calling itself the Inlet Public/Private Association took the lead in restoring the lighthouse in the late 1980s. In 1995, the group hired Sara Cureton as its executive director, making her the first lighthouse keeper since 1933. With grants totaling more than $1.6 million from a variety of sources, the association had the tower restored and opened it up to the public in 1999.

These photographs show the back end of Garden Pier, where the B. F. Keith's Theatre once stood. The boardwalk side had a more positive outcome. The Atlantic City Art Center opened in the early 1950s, with Florence Valore Miller appointed as its executive director in the 1960s. At the urging of Miller and councilman Walter Collette, the Atlantic City Historical Museum joined the art center in 1985. Together, the two museums offer a unique refuge from the glitz and schmaltz that has always marked Atlantic City. Also, admittance is free, in a city that has always looked for ways to pick people's pockets.

Five

RESURRECTION
1975–1995

City fathers and what was left of the tourist industry were not about to take no for an answer when it came to casinos. The issue appeared on the ballot in 1976, but this time, the focus limited casino gaming to Atlantic City. The voters approved the referendum. Unlike the illegal gambling prevalent in old Atlantic City, the state drafted extensive legislation to regulate casinos. The Mary Carter Paint Company rolled the first dice, buying the Chalfonte-Haddon Hall Hotel. The Chalfonte portion came down, but Haddon Hall opened as a casino hotel in 1978 with the uninspiring moniker, Resorts International. In the next several years, more casinos opened. A dozen casinos operated in 1990, the newest being Trump Taj Mahal. By then, Atlantic City's hotel resorts, bound in the early years by restrictions in design, looked tired. Gaming revenues kept climbing, so the industry focused little energy on creating Las Vegas-style megaresorts. In 1995, the first glimmers of change emerged.

Flanked by huge crowds and local officials, New Jersey governor Brendan Byrne signs the Casino Control Act in 1977. Joining Byrne was Steve Perskie, the local state senator who wrote the act, Mayor Joseph Lazarow, and former Republican boss, Frank "Hap" Farley, who worked behind the scenes to get gaming approved. The act laid out the regulations that would govern gaming in

Atlantic City and become the standard other states would follow in crafting similar legislation in years to come. The day he signed the law, Byrne issued this now famous warning to the mob: "I've said it before and I will repeat it again: Keep your filthy hands off Atlantic City! Keep the hell out of our state."

Resorts International opened the first casino at North Carolina Avenue and the boardwalk. Singer Steve Lawrence threw the first dice on the craps table to open the gaming era in Atlantic City. Huge crowds waited in long lines that stretched down the boardwalk for a chance to play slots and blackjack, even with a dress code that required visitors to wear jackets on the gaming floor. Jackets were available at the coat check concession. These crowds did not go unnoticed by the major gaming companies in Las Vegas.

In this image, Sammy Davis Jr. talks with Mayor Joseph Lazarow as he prepares to judge the Easter parade in 1979. Davis was long a fixture in Atlantic City, performing at Club Harlem and 500 Club in the old Atlantic City and in many of the casino showrooms in the new Atlantic City.

Clifford and Stuart Perlman, owners of Caesar's Palace in Las Vegas, bet on Atlantic City even before Resorts International opened its doors. Caesar's leased the 425-room Howard Johnson's Regency Motor Hotel at Arkansas Avenue and the boardwalk and planned a small tower to bring the number of rooms to 500, the legal minimum required by the state to operate a casino. Named Caesar's Boardwalk Regency, the new casino received a temporary license to open after Clifford Perlman gave up most of his connection with the property in light of allegations of being tied to the mob. Caesar's ended Resorts International's 11-month monopoly when it opened its doors in June 1979. This image shows the original Caesar's Boardwalk Regency from across Pacific Avenue. Lengthy hearings on a permanent license ended in the Perlmans' ouster from Caesar's Boardwalk Regency's corporate parent as a condition to continue operation in Atlantic City. In 1987, the Boardwalk Regency portion of the name disappeared, and the casino hotel became Caesar's Atlantic City. Caesar's had purchased the site of the former Traymore Hotel with plans to build a Caesar's Palace. It never happened, and the land remains a parking lot today.

The photograph shows Bally's Park Place under construction in 1979. Bally Manufacturing, after severing ties with executives who had a shadowy past, bought—and demolished—the Marlborough-Blenheim, but saved the Dennis Hotel. The company restored 507 rooms, enough to qualify for a license. They added a casino, restaurants, and a theater. It opened on December 30, 1979, as the third casino, as Caesar's Boardwalk Regency opened earlier in the year.

In 1989, Bally's Park Place opened the 800-room tower shown in this picture. Coupled with the rooms at the Dennis Hotel, Bally's Park Place became the first casino hotel in Atlantic City to have 1,000 rooms. In the foreground sits the facade of old Warner Theatre, retained in hopes of incorporating it into future casino hotel projects.

This image shows the Brighton Hotel Casino on the site of the old Brighton Hotel on Indiana Avenue. Built by the Greate Bay Casino Corporation, it was the first all-new casino hotel when it opened in August 1980. Bankruptcy rumors quickly swirled, and the Brighton was sold before year's end to the Pratt brothers, who had recently purchased the Sands in Las Vegas. In May 1981, the Brighton changed its name to the Sands, the same name it currently bears. As a casino hotel, the Sands has always been hampered by its location off the boardwalk. The hotel long coveted the former Traymore site leading to the boardwalk, but Caesar's Boardwalk Regency refused to sell. Once Harrah's Entertainment took over Caesars in 2005, the roadblock ended and the Sands's parent company acquired the site with an eye towards building a new casino hotel or selling everything to another operator.

The Claridge was one of the newest of the grand old hotels in Atlantic City when it opened in 1930. In 1979, a new life awaited the hotel, this time with a casino and a phalanx of restaurants. The actual name was Del Webb's Claridge Hotel and Hi-Ho Casino, a partnership between a Connecticut-based Claridge Associates and the Del Webb Corporation. Webb had a long history in the Las Vegas gaming market, building and owning a piece of Bugsy Siegel's Flamingo in Las Vegas. A pending conspiracy trial in Las Vegas forced Webb to shed some of its officials before the Division of Gaming Enforcement lifted its opposition to a license. The Claridge opened in July 1981. In the image below, gamblers play at one of the table games inside the casino.

Ramada Inns bought the Ambassador Hotel with the idea of renovating it into a casino resort. Those plans were denied by Gov. Brendan Byrne and the Casino Control Commission, who wanted new buildings, not the kind of patch jobs that marked Resorts, Bally's, and the Claridge. Ramada president M. William Isbell objected to the apparent double standard but in the end gave in. Construction began at a time when Ramada purchased the Tropicana in Las Vegas, and like the Sands owners, the company capitalized on the famous name. The Atlantic City Tropicana opened at Brighton Avenue and the boardwalk in November 1981.

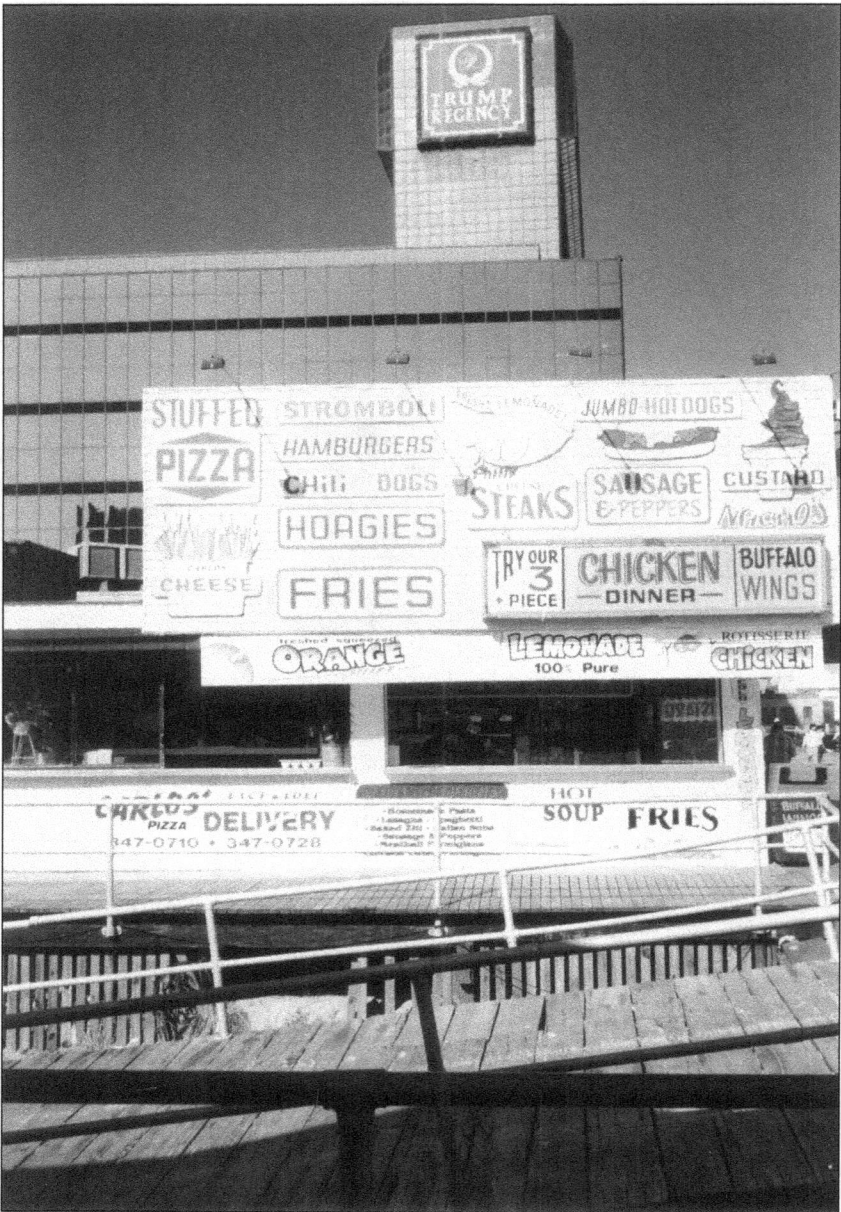

The Atlantis Casino Hotel was a case study in the various convolutions in the Atlantic City gaming world. Built as the Playboy Casino Hotel, authorities denied Hugh Hefner a permanent license a year after opening, over allegations of impropriety. Hefner sold his interest, and the property became the Atlantis. In 1989, the Atlantis held the distinction of being the first—and so far only—casino to shut down because of bankruptcy. Donald Trump took over, but because state regulations prohibited ownership of more than three casinos, he operated it as a hotel only, called Trump Regency, pictured here. When the state removed the three casino prohibition in 1996, Trump brought gaming back and renamed the hotel Trump World's Fair, an arm of Trump Plaza. Then in 1999, Trump shut down the money-losing Trump World's Fair and eventually demolished the building.

The newest of Trump's casinos in Atlantic City, the Trump Taj Mahal opened in 1990 at Virginia Avenue and the boardwalk. Trump acquired the partly finished building as part of a deal with Merv Griffin over control of Resorts International, which began the construction; Griffin received Resorts International and property in the Bahamas as a result. The casino hotel, with its Indian architecture, is the flagship of Trump's Atlantic City empire, and has one of the largest casino floors in the city. At night, the Taj appears as a neon fantasy world from the outside. Films such as *Snake Eyes* and *Rounders* had scenes shot at the Taj Mahal.

In 1993, Resorts International celebrated its 15th anniversary—and 15 years of successful casino gaming in Atlantic City. Steve Lawrence returned to toss the dice, as former New Jersey governor Brendan Byrne looked on. By then, a dozen of casinos were open for business. The industry won more than $3.3 billion in 1993.

Planet Hollywood was one of the first themed restaurants to open in Atlantic City. Founded by Arnold Schwarzeneggar, Bruce Willis, and Sylvester Stallone, the memorabilia-laden restaurant occupied prime real estate at Caesar's Atlantic City on the corner of Arkansas Avenue and the boardwalk. Willis and his band entertained on the boardwalk at its grand opening.

Six

RENAISSANCE
1996–2006

The renaissance of Atlantic City began when Steve Wynn announced plans to construct a lavish resort in the marina section of the city for almost $1 billion. He also promised that some of his Las Vegas friends would join the party. MGM Grand wanted in and proposed a similar development along the boardwalk. Talk has remained cheap in Atlantic City, however, where the number of proposed casinos clearly outweighs the actual number. Lawsuits and legal maneuverings delayed both projects. Then MGM Grand bought Wynn's company; the plans changed, Wynn and his megaresort were out. With title to land in the marina, MGM Grand, not bogged down by dealings with real estate speculators, dropped its boardwalk site to concentrate on the marina. Out of this emerged Borgata Hotel Casino and Spa, a joint venture between MGM Mirage and Boyd Gaming. Borgata opened in 2003 and transformed the resort again, bringing a fashionable taste of Las Vegas to Atlantic City. The $1.1 billion palace proved customers were willing to visit an Atlantic City with upscale rooms, top name chefs, and chic clubs. In the wake of Borgata's success, the Tropicana unveiled the Quarter, an old Havana-themed retail, dining, and entertainment attraction. Showboat brought in the House of Blues, and Caesar's converted the former Million Dollar Pier into a dazzling retail, dining, and entertainment extravaganza over the beach and ocean.

As the casinos redefined Atlantic City, life continued outside the gaming hall walls. The New Jersey Education Association (NJEA), the state teachers union and one of the oldest in the country, has held its annual convention in the resort since its founding in 1854. This image shows the floor at the convention hall with the exhibits during the NJEA convention.

Fralinger's Salt Water Taffy had been going strong since the company was founded in 1885. The association of salt water taffy with Atlantic City was just as true in the casino age. In this image, strollers walk by the store at Tennessee Avenue and the boardwalk.

Amid all the speculation over another makeover for Atlantic City, the White House Sub Shop celebrated its 50th birthday in 1996. The sandwich shop, an institution in Atlantic City, survived the deterioration and the rebirth of the city, and planned to survive the coming renaissance as well. Lines still snaked around the corner onto Mississippi Avenue. Like other restaurants that predate gaming in the resort—the Knife and Fork Inn, Dock's Oyster House, Tony's Baltimore Grill, Angelo's Fairmount Tavern, and the Irish Pub, to name a handful—little had changed in half a century. The inside of the White House is like a trip down memory lane. The furnishings remain the same, highlighted by photographs of famous visitors such as the Beatles, Bill Cosby, and Frank Sinatra. Enthusiasts have been known to have their favorite sub shipped around the country.

Borgata Hotel Casino and Spa, its exterior shown here, turned the tide in Atlantic City and set the stage for the future. Boyd Gaming Corporation, the Las Vegas owners of the Stardust, saw Borgata and its 2,000 rooms as its flagship property. The goal of CEO Robert Boughner was to create a resort that would overcome the objections many visitors had toward coming to Atlantic City. Even the standard rooms were large, and the decor and accoutrements were top grade. Boughner brought in the famed Old Homestead Steak House, long a fixture in New York City. From Philadelphia, he tapped Susanna Foo, who opened a Chinese restaurant, Suilan. Chef Luke Palladino opened two restaurants, Specchio and Ombra. Borgata included hip nightspots such as the Gypsy Bar, just off the casino floor, and the sensual mixx was a Latin-Asian restaurant in the early evening and a hot dance club with private rooms at night. The marketing reached out for segments often ignored by the competition. The company placed advertisements in high-end glossy magazines, and this effort did not go unnoticed.

The top image in one of the corridors shows the Dale Chihuly chandeliers and sculptures decorated throughout Borgata Hotel Casino and Spa, one of the many decorative touches employed when the property opened. Borgata also brought back sensual cocktail servers known as Borgata Babes who patrolled the casino floor, shown in the background. Noodles of the World, whose entrance is shown in the image to the right, is a noodle bar on the actual casino floor. Noodles of the World features a variety of noodle options from Thailand, Japan, China, Vietnam, and Korea, as well as other quick-meal Asian delicacies.

Survival in Atlantic City meant expansion and name changes—and still does. Bally's Park Place morphed into Bally's Atlantic City and expects to receive a new name, one which will drop Bally's. The top image of Bally's shows a new parking garage associated with Caesar's Atlantic City. Caesar's has since opened a hotel tower and another parking garage, with plans for more hotel rooms on the drawing board. Elsewhere, Tropicana has added a couple of towers to meet the growing demand for rooms. So did Resorts International, Showboat, Hilton, and Harrah's. The bottom image shows a new facade on the boardwalk entrance to Bally's.

The Showboat opened in 1987 with its highlight, a huge bowling center similar to the one it had in Las Vegas. Bowling never really caught on in Atlantic City, and the center gave way to new restaurants. The company also built a couple of new hotel towers. This aerial image shows the Showboat, the ocean in the background.

In 2005, the Showboat transformed its boardwalk frontage into a House of Blues, shown here. The famed club, founded by Dan Aykroyd, includes the Music Hall, a dance club, a smaller concert area named Club Harlem (in deference to the legendary Atlantic City nightspot), and the chain's largest Foundation Room, a members-only upscale restaurant and club decorated with Asian, Indian, and African art.

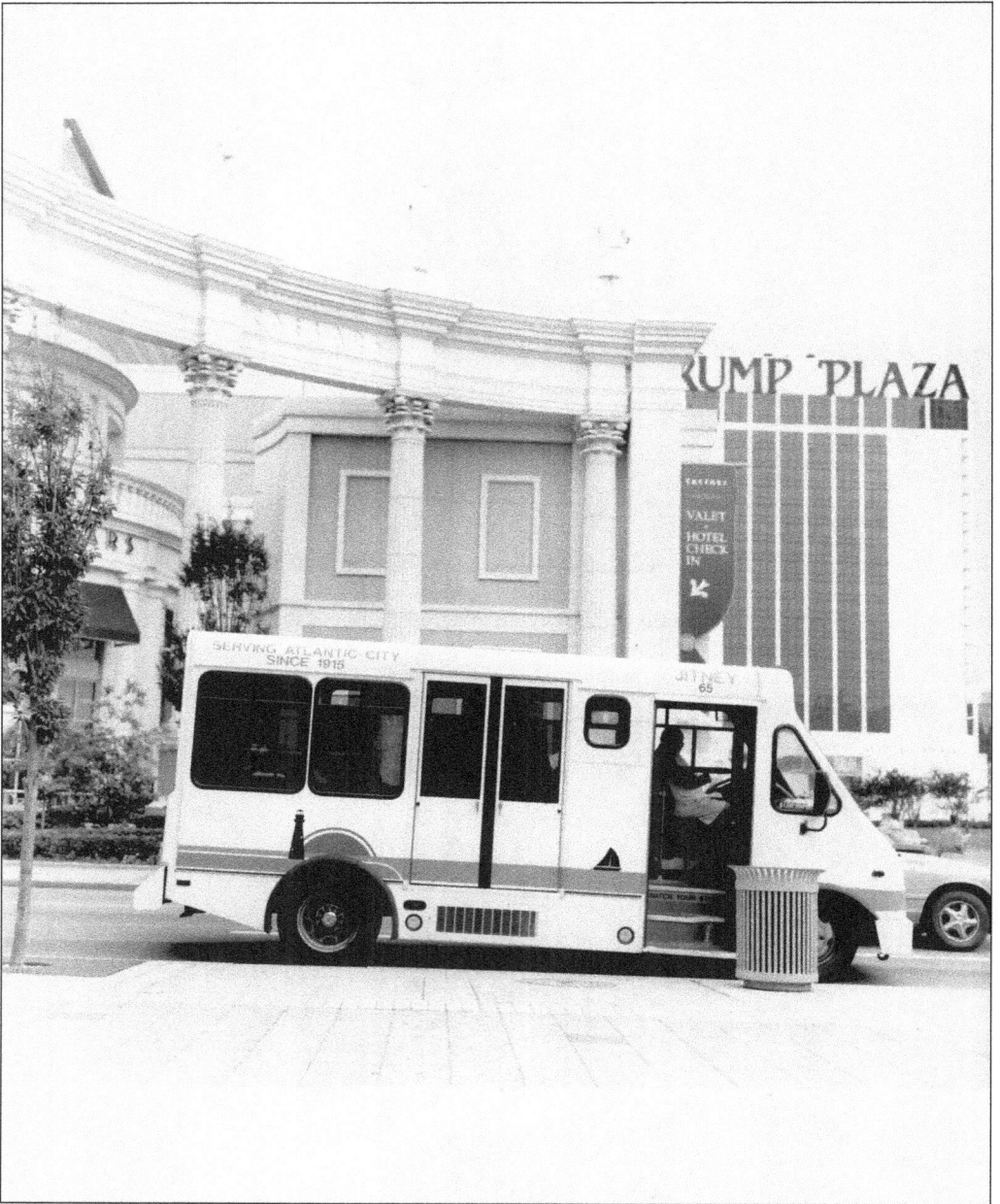

In the early years of the 21st century, the jitney got a new look, thanks to an investment from the Casino Reinvestment Development Authority. The larger, more modern coaches still carry the same number of seats. The number of jitney licenses remains at 190, as it has almost since the inception of jitney service in 1915; only the fare and the number of routes had changed.

The Atlantic City International Airport lies 10 miles from the boardwalk and adjacent to the William J. Hughes Federal Aviation Administration's technical center. This technical center houses research on aviation, and much of it is tried out on the immense runways at the airport. Gaming brought a growth of charter flights full of gamblers and commercial flights to and from Florida and other destinations. The image above is a shot of the exterior of the airport terminal. The image below shows Spirit Airlines jets. Spirit, which began life by flying in gamblers on charters from Detroit, now accounts for some 75 percent of the commercial traffic.

This image shows one of two plazas that are the focal points of The Quarter, Tropicana's centerpiece that opened in 2004. The project was delayed nine months after a tragic construction accident killed four workers. The Quarter, designed to resemble an Old Havana street scene, features high-end retail shops, restaurants, and clubs. Restaurants shown here include P. F. Chang's, Red Square, and Cuba Libre, offering Chinese, Russian, and Cuban delicacies. The Quarter offers visitors plenty of options outside the casino. Indeed, the attraction is accessed without even seeing a slot machine.

In 2007, Borgata Hotel Casino and Spa is set to open the Water Club, shown here in a rendering. The 800-room tower comes four years after Borgata opened its doors for the first time and a year after an expansion that brought in restaurants by Wolfgang Puck, Michael Mina, and Bobby Flay. The Water Club features four swimming pools and its own spa.

Harrah's Atlantic City has also committed to a new tower of its own, which will be its fourth. The 964-room tower is set to open in 2008, including a Red Door Salon and other amenities. Harrah's parent company, Harrah's Entertainment, is committed to constructing another tower at Bally's Atlantic City and at Caesar's Atlantic City. In 2006, the Pier at Caesar's opened across the boardwalk from Caesar's on the site that once housed Million Dollar Pier.

This image depicts a rendering of the new tower at the Trump Taj Mahal, standing adjacent to the existing tower. For years, Donald Trump's casino empire—Trump Plaza, Trump Marina, and Trump Taj Mahal—faced financial problems, leading to a bankruptcy. A lack of funding prevented the company from expanding and adding the kind of amenities demanded by the new visitor to Atlantic City. Once the courts approved a reorganization plan in 2005, Trump had the money to spend and went forward with a long-delayed proposal to build a much-needed hotel tower at the Taj. The 800-room tower is expected rise 45 stories and cost $250 million when it opens in 2008. Long-range plans call for additional towers at Trump Plaza and Trump Marina and possibly refashioning Steel Pier from an amusement park into a retail, dining, and entertainment attraction.

INDEX

Visit us at
arcadiapublishing.com

www.ingramcontent.com/pod-product-compliance
Lightning Source LLC
Chambersburg PA
CBHW080554110426
42813CB00006B/1307